Godfrey Golding

How to get on, being the book of good devices

A thousand precepts for practice

Godfrey Golding

How to get on, being the book of good devices
A thousand precepts for practice

ISBN/EAN: 9783742833587

Manufactured in Europe, USA, Canada, Australia, Japa

Cover: Foto ©Lupo / pixelio.de

Manufactured and distributed by brebook publishing software (www.brebook.com)

Godfrey Golding

How to get on, being the book of good devices

"FULL OF NOBLE DEVICE."—*Shakespeare.*

HOW TO GET ON:

BEING

THE BOOK OF GOOD DEVICES.

A Thousand Precepts for Practice.

EDITED BY

GODFREY GOLDING.

Third Edition.

CASSELL, PETTER & GALPIN:
LONDON, PARIS & NEW YORK.

"RICH AND OF DEVICEFUL THREAD."—*Chapman.*

If thou wouldst keep from disorder,

Preface.

"A Book of Good Devices may very reasonably demand attention and acceptance from those that have any impressions of the most reasonable religion upon them." So wrote Dr. Cotton Mather, in his famous "Essays to do Good," which were so highly spoken of by Benjamin Franklin.

The idea of the present volume was suggested by this remark; and in it the Editor has endeavoured to gather together, for the guidance and edification of youth, the opinions and experiences of eminent men, esteemed for their piety, patriotism, and wisdom, or famed for their commercial success and practical knowledge of every-day life.

The object of the Editor has been to select such passages from the writings of the authors here

By love serve one another.

Commit thy way unto the Lord.

Curb thy desires.

Be discreet in your discourse,

represented, as convey distinct religious, moral, or practical lessons, valuable and important in themselves, and within the comprehension of the youthful readers for whom they are intended. A wide range of subjects has been selected, and occasionally the same matters are treated by two or more authors. The experiences narrated or conclusions arrived at, in several cases, do not correspond; but it is, nevertheless, interesting and important to observe in what varied aspects the same subject may be viewed by different writers, while their several deductions may be equally valuable.

The wise, terse, and pithy proverbial PRECEPTS FOR PRACTICE which encompass each page contain many valuable lessons, which, from their brevity and conciseness of expression, readily commend themselves, and can be easily committed to memory, where they may be retained as moral ammunition for service in every department of future life.

The BOOK OF GOOD DEVICES is offered to all who interest themselves in the welfare of youth, and who desire, by means of counsel and advice, to

But more in your actions:

Let your example be the Son of man.

protect them from the many snares and temptations which beset them on their entrance to, and in their progress through life, more especially those in large towns and great cities.

In the words of Dr. Mather, who has been already referred to, the Editor commends the BOOK OF GOOD DEVICES to all concerned, as "full of reasonable and serviceable things; and it would be well for us if such things were regarded."

⁎ The Editor of "THE BOOK OF GOOD DEVICES" desires to thank SAMUEL SMILES, Esq., for permission, readily granted, to make use of passages from his admirable and valuable books for youth, "Character" and "Self-Help;" and Messrs. STRAHAN and Co., for the like favour from Principal TULLOCH'S "Beginning Life."

NOTE.—The First Edition of this Work was published under the title of "The Book of Good Devices."

A wise man's heart is at his right hand;

But a fool's is at his left.

See that ye refuse not Him that speaketh.

A good maxim

Mercy and truth shall be to them

That devise good.

My son, if thou wilt receive my words,
And hide my commandments with thee;
So that thou incline thine ear unto wisdom
And apply thine heart to understanding;
Yea, if thou criest after knowledge,
And liftest up thy voice for understanding;
If thou seekest her as silver,
And searchest for her as for hid treasures;
Then shalt thou understand the fear of the Lord,
And find the knowledge of God.

Is never out of season.

A wise son maketh a glad father:

THE
BOOK OF GOOD DEVICES.

SIR HENRY SIDNEY TO HIS SON.

LET your first action be the lifting up of your mind to Almighty God, by hearty prayer, and feelingly digest the words you speak in prayer, with continual meditation, and thinking of Him to whom you pray, and of the matter for which you pray. And use this as an ordinary, and at an ordinary hour; whereby the time itself will put you in remembrance to do that which you are accustomed to do. In that time apply your study to such hours as your discreet master doth assign you, earnestly; and the time he will so limit, as shall be both sufficient for your learning and safe for your health. And mark the sense and the matter of that you read, as well as the words. So shall you both enrich your tongue with words, and your wit with matter; and judgment will grow as your years

But a foolish son is the heaviness of his mother.

Hear the instruction of thy father.

Forsake not the law of thy mother.

Be temperate in all things.

groweth with you. Be humble and obedient to your master, for unless you frame yourself to obey others, yea, and feel in yourself what obedience is, you shall never be able to teach others how to obey you.

Be courteous of gesture, and affable to all men, with diversity of reverence, according to the dignity of the person. There is nothing that winneth so much with so little cost. Use moderate diet, so that after your meat you may find your wit fresher, and not duller, and your body more lively, and not more heavy. Seldom drink wine, and yet sometimes do, lest being enforced to drink upon the sudden, you should find yourself inflamed. Use exercise of body, but such as is without peril of your joints or bones. It will increase your force and enlarge your breath. Delight to be cleanly, as well in all parts of your body, as in your garments. It shall make you grateful in each company, and otherwise loathsome. Give yourself to be merry, for you degenerate from your father if you find not yourself most able in wit and body to do anything, when you be most merry: but let your mirth be ever void of all scurrility, and biting words to any man; for a wound given by a word is oftentimes harder to be cured than that which is given with the sword. Be you rather a hearer and bearer away of other men's talk, than a beginner or procurer of speech, otherwise you shall be counted to

A blustering man is a coward.

The tongue is an unruly member.

delight to hear yourself speak. If you hear a wise sentence, or an apt phrase, commit it to your memory, with respect of the circumstance, when you shall speak it.

Let never oath be heard to come out of your mouth, nor word of ribaldry; detest it in others, so shall custom make to yourself a law against it in yourself. Be modest in each assembly, and rather be rebuked of light fellows for maiden-like shamefacedness, than of your sad friends for pert boldness. Think upon every word that you will speak, before you utter it; and remember how nature hath rampired up, as it were, the tongue with the teeth, lips, yea, and hair without the lips, and all betokening reins, or bridles, for the loose use of that member.

Above all things, tell no untruth, no, not in trifles. The custom of it is naughty; and let it not satisfy you that, for a time, the hearers take it for a truth; for after, it will be known as it is to your shame; for there cannot be a greater reproach to a gentleman than to be accounted a liar. Study and endeavour yourself to be virtuously occupied. So shall you make such an habit of well-doing in you, that you shall not know how to do evil, though you would.

SIR HENRY SIDNEY.

Apply thine heart to understanding.

Trust in the Lord with all thy might.

All lies disgrace a gentleman.

The Lord giveth wisdom.

MAN.

How poor! how rich! how abject! how august!
How complicate! how wonderful is Man!
How passing wond'rous He who made him such!
Who centred in our make such strange extremes!
From different natures marvellously mixt,
Connection exquisite of distant worlds!
Distinguish'd link in being's endless chain!
Midway from nothing to the Deity!
A beam ethereal sullied, and absorb'd!
Though sullied and dishonour'd, still divine!
Dim miniature of greatness absolute!
An heir of glory! a frail child of dust!
Helpless immortal! insect infinite!
A worm! a god! I tremble at myself,
And in myself am lost! at home a stranger,
Thought wanders up and down, surpris'd, aghast,
And wond'ring at her own: how reason reels!
O what a miracle is man to man!
Triumphantly distress'd, what joy, what dread!
Alternately transported and alarm'd!
What can preserve my life? or what destroy?
An angel's arm can't snatch me from the grave;
Legions of angels can't confine me there.

EDWARD YOUNG.

A wise man will hear and increase learning.

The Lord is a buckler to them that walk uprightly.

Remove thy feet from evil.

A good man is a common good.

Doing Good.

HOW much evil may be done by one wicked man! Yea, sometimes one wicked man, of slender abilities, becoming an indefatigable tool of the devil, may do an incredible mischief in the world. We have seen some wretched instruments of cursed memory ply the intention of doing mischief at a strange rate, till they have undone a whole country; yea, unto the undoing of more than three kingdoms. It is a melancholy consideration, and I may say, an astonishing one; you will hardly find one of a thousand who does half so much to serve God and Christ and his own soul, as you may see done by thousands to serve the devil. A horrible thing!

We read of a man "who deviseth mischief upon his bed; who setteth himself in a way that is not good." Now, why should not we be as active, as frequent, as forward in devising good, and as full of exquisite contrivances? Why should not we be as wise to do good as any are to do evil? I am sure we have a better cause, and better reason for it. My friend—though perhaps thou art one who makest but a little figure in the world, "a brother of low degree," yet behold a vast encouragement. A little man may do a great deal of harm; and, pray, why

A good name is rather to be chosen than great riches.

A good name is the reward of goodness.

Strive to do good unto all men.

Wise men lay up knowledge.

may not a little man do a great deal of good? It is possible "the wisdom of a poor man" may start a proposal which may "save a city"—serve a nation!

A single hair, applied to a flyer that has other wheels depending on it, may pull up an oak, or pull down a house.

COTTON MATHER.

THE BEGINNING OF WISDOM.

IT was the wisest saying of the wisest man, the fear of God is the beginning of wisdom. Holiness, then, is the introduction of all wisdom, so it shall be the first of my advice. Fear God, and if holiness give knowledge, knowledge will give thee happiness, long life, riches, and honour. Length of days is in the right hand of wisdom, and in her left hand are riches and honour. How exalted a thing, then, is religion, which is the mother of so great blessings, and who will pity thy complaints for the want of any of these, if they be obtained by the pleasure of that which will also crown thee with heaven, an holy life; be pious, and thou art all these; fear God, and thou shalt not fear man or devil, for it will set thee above the reach of fortune or malice.

EARL OF BEDFORD.

The end of learning is to know God.

AGAINST FLATTERY.

TAKE care thou be not made a fool by flatterers, for even the wisest men are abused by these. Know, therefore, that flatterers are the worst kind of traitors; for they will strengthen thy imperfections, encourage thee in all evils, correct thee in nothing; but so shadow and paint all thy vices and follies, as thou shalt never, by their will, discern evil from good, or vice from virtue. And because all men are apt to flatter themselves, to entertain the additions of other men's praises is most perilous. Do not, therefore, praise thyself, except thou wilt be counted a vainglorious fool; neither take delight in the praises of other men, except thou deserve it, and receive it from such as are worthy and honest, and will withal warn thee of thy faults; for flatterers have never any virtue; they are ever base, creeping, cowardly persons. A flatterer is said to be a beast that biteth smiling; it is said by Isaiah in this manner:—*My people, they that praise thee, seduce thee, and disorder the paths of thy feet;* and David desired God to cut out the tongue of a flatterer. But it is hard to know them from friends, they are so obsequious and full of protestations; for as a wolf resembleth a dog, so doth a flatterer a friend. A flatterer is compared to an ape,

Buy the truth, and sell it not.

who, because she cannot defend the house like a dog, labour as an ox, or bear burdens as a horse, doth therefore yet play tricks, and provoke laughter. Thou mayest be sure that he that will in private tell thee thy faults is thy friend, for he adventures thy dislike, and doth hazard thy hatred; for there are few men that can endure it, every man for the most part delighting in self-praise, which is one of the most universal follies that bewitcheth mankind.

SIR WALTER RALEIGH.

THE HEIGHT OF HONOUR.

No man to offend—
Ne'er to reveal the secrets of a friend;
Rather to suffer, than to do a wrong,
To make the heart no stranger to the tongue;
Provoked, not to betray an enemy,
Nor at his meat I choke with flattery;
Blushless to tell wherefore I wear my scars,
Or for my conscience, or my country's wars;
To aim at just things; if we've wildly run
Into offences, wish them all undone;
'Tis poor, in grief for a wrong done, to die—
Honour to dare to live, and satisfy.

MASSINGER.

Before honour is humility.

They that praise thee, seduce thee.

Be not wise in thine own eyes.

Choose your friends with care.

On the Choice of Friends.

THERE is nothing more becoming any wise man than to make choice of friends, for by them thou shalt be judged what thou art. Let them, therefore, be wise and virtuous, and none of these that follow thee for gain; but make election rather of thy betters than thy inferiors, shunning always such as are poor and needy; for, if thou givest twenty gifts, and refuse to do the like but once, all that thou hast done will be lost, and such men will become thy mortal enemies. Take also special care that thou never trust any friend or servant with any matter that may endanger thine estate, for so shalt thou make thyself a bond-slave to him that thou trustest, and leave thyself always to his mercy; and be sure of this, thou shalt never find a friend in thy young years whose conditions and qualities will please thee after thou comest to more discretion and judgment, and then all thou givest is lost, and all wherein thou shalt trust such a one will be discovered. Such, therefore, as are thy inferiors will follow thee but to eat of thee, and when thou leavest to feed them they will hate thee; and such kind of men, if thou preserve thy estate, will always be had. And if thy friends be of better quality than thyself,

He that walketh with wise men shall be wise.

thou mayest be sure of two things: the first, that they will be more careful to keep thy counsel, because they have more to lose than thou hast; the second, they will esteem thee for thyself, and not for that which thou dost possess. But if thou be subject to any great vanity or ill, then therein trust no man; for every man's folly ought to be his greatest secret. And, although I persuade thee to associate thyself with thy betters, or at least with thy peers, yet remember always that thou venture not thy estate with any of those great ones that shall attempt unlawful things; for such men labour for themselves, and not for thee; thou shalt be sure to part with them in the danger, but not in the honour; and to venture a sure estate in present, in hope of a better in future, is mere madness: and great men forget such as have done them service when they have obtained what they would, and will rather hate thee for saying thou hast been a means of their advancement than acknowledge it.

When thou shalt read and observe the "Stories of all Nations," thou shalt find innumerable examples of the like. Let thy love be to the best, so long as they do well; but take heed that thou love God, thy country, thy prince, and thine own estate before all others: for the fancies of men change, and he that loves to-day hateth to-morrow; but let reason be thy schoolmistress, which shall ever guide thee right.

SIR WALTER RALEIGH.

First impressions are lasting.

YOUTHFUL IMPRESSIONS.

THE impression that every man makes upon his age and country is not so much determined by the events and associations of his manhood, as by the ruling principles or passions of his boyhood and youth; so that youth is the bud of which manhood is the flower; and, as it were, the present is the faithful type and prophet of the most distant future.

It is an eventful moment when the masterpiece of the sculptor's skill is being cast in the mould, for soon it shall harden, and whatever be its faults or its virtues, it must go down to posterity unchanged. It is an hour of thrilling interest when a nation's destinies hang trembling in the balance, and a word or act may shape them for unborn generations. But, oh! where, in the case of an individual, is there a period so eventful, so fraught with tremendous consequences for good or evil, as when the youth pauses upon the threshold of active life, and yields his plastic mind to the abiding impress of truth or error, and forms those habits which shall be interwoven with the whole texture of his coming existence?

Could the young man who is disposed to trifle with solemn truth have the future unveiled to his view, and see this or that evil practice embittering a

The boy is father of the man.

Honest youth makes happy age.

Youth is the season of promise.

Get wisdom.

career that is now so full of hope—see the silken threads of sinful pleasure turning into cords that shall strangle his soul's life—see the luxuriant harvest of disgrace, poverty, wretchedness, that shall spring from the seeds he so recklessly sows, he would surely be aroused to sober reflection. Or could he who now struggles successfully against temptation, look beyond the present conflict and victory, and trace their beneficent effects upon the confirmed principles of manhood and old age, he would surely be inspired with fresh strength, nor think the most hard-earned conquest dearly bought.

Let this thought, then, be lodged deeply in every youthful mind, that NOW is the crisis of life—that every hour of time, every habit of thought, feeling, or action, the book or paper you read, the words you hear, the companions you associate with, the purposes you cherish—each makes its indelible mark, and all combine and work together in forming you for future honour, usefulness, and happiness, or for shame, misery, and death. COLLYER.

AVOIDING evil is but one half of our work; we must also do good. One act of beneficence, one act of real usefulness, is worth all the abstract sentiment in the world, and that humanity is despicable which can be contented to pity where it might assuage.

Resist the devil, and he will flee from you.

Enter not into the path of the wicked.

Hear instruction, and be wise.

REMEMBER THE POOR.

TAKE heed that thou seek not riches basely nor attain them by evil means; destroy no man for his wealth, nor take anything from the poor; for the cry and complaint thereof will pierce the heavens. And it is most detestable before God, and most dishonourable before worthy men, to wrest anything from the needy and labouring soul. God will never prosper thee in aught if thou offend therein; but use thy poor neighbours and tenants well, pine not them and their children to add superfluity and needless expenses to thyself. He that hath pity on another man's sorrow shall be free from it himself; and he that delighteth in and scorneth the misery of another, shall one time or other fall into it himself. Remember this precept, "He that hath mercy on the poor, lendeth unto the Lord, and the Lord will recompense him what he hath given." I do not understand those for poor which are vagabonds and beggars, but those that labour to live, such as are old and cannot travel, such poor widows and fatherless children as are ordered to be relieved, and the poor tenants that travail to pay their rents, and are driven to poverty by mischance, and not by riot or careless expenses; on such have thou compassion, and God will bless thee for it. Make

God hateth false lips.

not the hungry soul sorrowful, defer not thy gift to the needy; for if he curse thee in the bitterness of his soul, his prayer shall be heard of Him that made him.　　　　　　　　　　SIR WALTER RALEIGH.

FALSEHOOD.

TAKE heed that thou be not found a liar; for a lying spirit is hateful both to God and man. A liar is commonly a coward, for he dares not avow truth. A liar is trusted of no man, he can have no credit, either in public or private; and if there were no more arguments than this, know that our Lord, in St. John, saith that *it is a vice proper to Satan*, lying being opposite to the nature of God, which consisteth in truth; and the gain of lying is nothing else, but not to be trusted of any, nor to be believed when we say the truth. It is said in the Proverbs that *God hateth false lips; and he that speaketh lies shall perish*. Thus thou mayest see and find in all the books of God, how odious and contrary to God a liar is; and for the world, believe it, that it never did any man good, except in the extremity of saving life, for a liar is of a base, unworthy, and cowardly spirit.

　　　　　　　　　　SIR WALTER RALEIGH.

Truth is truth, to the end of time.

Tell truth, and shame the devil.

He that speaketh lies shall perish.

Let us do good unto all men.

LIVE FOR OTHERS.

MAN never was intended to live only for himself, and therefore it is that no man can be happy who lives for himself. The one proposition flows necessarily from the other; for man, out of the path in which God has formed for him to walk, must be unhappy and constrained; as the bird, formed to soar towards the sun, would be miserable if tied, with clipped wings and fettered feet, to the ground; or as the seraph, formed for the atmosphere of holiness and praise, would change his songs to sighings if condemned to walk the thorny path of human life.

Let it then be settled in every mind that the fundamental law of all social relationship is to be found in the dictates of a kind, benevolent heart, that wishes well to all and evil to none; that prompts alike the friendly word and courteous demeanour, and that goes to make up what nothing else can either make or successfully counterfeit—the true gentleman. With this as a basis, one will scarcely require any other special rules for his guidance than that all-inclusive one of the Gospel, "As ye would that men should do unto you, do ye even so unto them."

He who obeys this will ever be on the alert to

Obey the golden rule.

Be not thou envious against evil men.

None of us liveth to himself.

As ye would that men should do to you,

impart, as well as to receive; to confer benefits, as well as to enjoy them; and in conferring to enjoy them all the more. As the heavenly bodies, moving harmoniously through space, reflect upon one another the light that warms them, so we, each in our orbit, whether as stars of greater or lesser magnitude, are to regard ourselves as charged with a mission to every one with whom we associate; our chief question being, not, How may I derive comfort or happiness? but, How may I cause other hearts to sing for joy?—not, How many blessings may I pluck for myself from the boughs that overhang life's way-side? but, How many may I disseminate? Some persons are like the gaudy, odourless flowers of the tropics, in which all the fertilising influences of sun and earth go into brilliant outward show, pleasing to the eye, but nothing more. Others resemble the blossoms of our orchards, with their modest purity of garb and colour, yet blessing all with the fragrance which they exhale, and then only dying to turn into fruit for man, as if their motto were, "None of us liveth to himself, and none dieth to himself." Would that this motto might be inscribed upon the opening portals of every youthful life.

COLLYER.

Do ye also to them.

He that hateth suretyship is sure.

SURETYSHIP.

AMONGST all other things of the world, take care of thy estate, which thou shalt ever preserve, if thou observe three things: first, that thou know what thou hast; what everything is worth that thou hast; and to see that thou art not wasted by thy servants and officers. The second is, that thou never spend anything before thou have it; for borrowing is the canker and death of every man's estate. The third is, that thou suffer not thyself to be wounded for other men's faults, and scourged for other men's offences; which is the surety for another; for thereby millions of men have been beggared and destroyed, paying the reckoning of other men's riot, and the charge of other men's folly and prodigality. If thou smart, smart for thine own sins, and, above all things, be not made an ass to carry the burdens of other men. If any desire thee to be his surety, give him a part of what thou hast to spare; if he press thee farther, he is not thy friend at all, for friendship rather chooseth harm to itself than offereth it. If thou be bound for a stranger, thou art a fool; if for a merchant, thou puttest thy estate to learn to swim; if for a church-man, he hath no inheritance; if for a lawyer, he will find an evasion, by a syllable or word, to abuse thee; if for a poor man, thou must

By suretyship a man maketh enemies.

Confess debt, and crave days.

The cautioner oft-times pays the debt.

Poverty is no crime.

pay it thyself; if for a rich man, he needs not: therefore, from suretyship, as from a man-slayer or enchanter, keep thyself; for the best profit and return will be this—that if thou force him for whom thou art bound to pay it himself, he will become thy enemy; if thou pay it thyself, thou wilt become a beggar. And believe thy father in this, and print it in thy thought—that what virtue soever thou hast, be it never so manifold, if thou be poor withal, thou and thy qualities shall be despised: besides, poverty is oftentimes sent as a curse of God, it is a shame amongst men, an imprisonment of the mind, a vexation of every worthy spirit. Thou shalt neither help thyself nor others; thou shalt drown thee in all thy virtues, having no means to show them; thou shalt be a burden and an eye-sore to thy friends; every man will fear thy company; thou shalt be driven basely to beg, and depend on others, to flatter unworthy men, to make dishonest shifts: and, to conclude, poverty provokes a man to do infamous and detested deeds. Let not vanity, therefore, or persuasion draw thee to that worst of worldly miseries.

If thou be rich, it will give thee pleasure in health, comfort in sickness, keep thy mind and body free, save thee from many perils, relieve thee in thy elder years, relieve the poor and thy honest friends, and give means to thy posterity to live and defend them-

Poor and content, is rich and rich enough.

The ready penny is the best friend.

Poverty is a hard taskmaster.

selves and thine own fame. Where it is said in the Proverbs that "he shall be sore vexed that is surety for a stranger, and he that hateth suretyship is sure :" it is farther said, "the poor is hated even of his own neighbour, but the rich have many friends." Lend not to him that is mightier than thyself, for if thou lendest him count it but lost. Be not surety above thy power, for if thou be surety think to pay it.

SIR WALTER RALEIGH.

Idle Jesting.

BE not scurrilous in conversation, nor satirical in thy jests. The one will make thee unwelcome to all company; the other pull on quarrels, and get thee hatred of thy best friends. For suspicious jests, when any of them savour of truth, leave a bitterness in the minds of those which are touched. I think it necessary to give this to thee as a special caution; because I have seen many so prone to quip and gird as they would rather lose their friend than their jest. And if perchance their boiling brain yield a quaint scoff, they will travail to be delivered of it as a woman with child. These nimble fancies are but the froth of wit.

LORD BURLEIGH.

Dare to do right. Nothing can need a lie;

Do Right.

DARE to do right—dare to be singular, if needs be, though the finger of scorn be pointed at you, and your spirit chafes under your comrades' sneers or laughter. Let it be enough that God smiles upon you—dare to strip off sin's artful disguises, to despise its hollow mockeries, to lay open its shallow pretences, and to make your face as adamant against its wiles and its threats—dare to go forth to battle with the Goliaths of evil, though they be of giant stature, and their spears like weavers' looms, and they defy in swelling words the armies of Israel; for the stripling David, with his sling and stone, shall conquer them in the name of the Lord of hosts. Be valiant for the truth, patient under oppression, meek under injury, strong in the anointing Spirit of God; and then the great social evils that we now deplore shall be slain, the better day shall dawn upon the human brotherhood, and the glad reign of love, virtue, peace, and holiness, for which men have so long waited, shall bless this weary world.

COLLYER.

There shall no evil happen to the just.

Blessings are upon the head of the just.

A fault that needs one most, grows two thereby.

'Tis education forms the common mind,

APHORISMS ON EDUCATION.

I. Let not an over-passionate prosecution of learning draw you from making an honest improvement of your estate; as such do who are better read in the bigness of the earth than that little spot left them by their friends for their support.

II. A mixed education suits employment best.

III. Huge volumes, like the ox roasted at Bartholomew Fair, may proclaim plenty of labour and invention, afford less of what is delicate, savoury, and well-concocted than smaller pieces: this makes me think that though, upon occasion, you may come to the table, and examine the bill of fare set down by such authors; yet it cannot but lessen ingenuity, still to fall aboard with them; human sufficiency being too narrow to inform, with the pure soul of reason, such vast bodies.

IV. As the grave hides the faults of physic, no less than mistakes, opinion and contrary applications are known to have enriched the art withal; so many old books, by like advantages rather than desert, have crawled up to an esteem above new: it being the business of better heads perhaps than ever their writers owned, to put a glorious and significant gloss upon the meanest conceit or improbable opinion of antiquity: whereas modern authors are brought by critics to a

Just as the twig is bent, the tree's inclined.

Apply thine heart to instruction.

Whoso loveth instruction loveth knowledge.

strict account for the smallest semblance of a mistake. If you consider this seriously, it will learn you more moderation, if not wisdom.

V. When I consider with what contradiction reports arrived at us, during our late civil wars, I can give the less encouragement to the reading of history: romances, never acted, being born purer from sophistication than actions reported to be done, by which posterity hereafter, no less than antiquity heretofore, is likely to be led into a false, or at best but a contingent, belief. Cæsar, though in this happy, that he had a pen able to grave into neat language what his sword at first more roughly cut out, may, in my judgment, abuse his reader; for he that, for the honour of his own wit, doth make people speak better than can be supposed men so barbarously bred were able, may possibly report they fought worse than really they did. Of a like value are the orations of Thucydides, Livy, Tacitus, and most other historians; which doth not a little prejudice all the rest.

VI. A few books well studied, and thoroughly digested, nourish the understanding more than hundreds but gargled in the mouth, as ordinary students use.

VII. Company, if good, is a better refiner of spirits than ordinary books.

VIII. Propose not them for patterns who make all places rattle where they come with Latin and Greek;

There is no darkness but ignorance.

for the more you seem to have borrowed from books, the poorer you proclaim your natural parts, which only can properly be called yours.

IX. Follow not the tedious practice of such as seek wisdom only in learning, not attainable but by experience and natural parts. Much reading, like a too great repletion, stopping up, through a concourse of diverse, sometimes contrary opinions, the access of a nearer, newer, and quicker invention of your own. And for quotations, they resemble sugar in wine, marring the natural taste of the liquor, if it be good; if bad, that of itself; such patches rather making the rent seem greater, by an interruption of the style, than less, if not so neatly applied as to fall in without drawing: nor is any thief in this kind sufferable, who comes not off, like a Lacedemonian, without discovery.

X. The way to elegancy of style is to employ your pen upon every errand; and the more trivial and dry it is, the more brains must be allowed for sauce: thus by checking all ordinary invention, your reason will attain to such a habit, as not to dare to present you but with what is excellent; and if void of affection, it matters not how mean the subject is: there being the same exactness observed, by good architects, in the structure of a kitchen as a parlour.

XI. When business or compliment calls you to write letters, consider what is fit to be said were the party present, and set down that.

Education is the best legacy.

Fools hate knowledge.

XII. Long experience has taught me that writers, for the most part, spend their money and time in the purchase of reproof and censure from envious contemporaries, or self-conceited posterity.

XIII. Be not frequent in poetry, how excellent however your vein is, but make it rather your recreation than business; because, though it swells you in your own opinion, it may render you less in that of wiser men, who are not ignorant how great a mass of vanity for the most part coucheth under this quality, proclaiming their heads like ships of use only for pleasure, and so richer in trimming than in lading.

XIV. It is incident to many, but as it were natural with poets, to think others take the like pleasure in hearing as they do in reading their own inventions. Not considering that the generality of ears are commonly stopped with prejudice of ignorance: neither can the understandings of men, any more than their tastes, be wooed to find a like savour in all things; one approving what others condemn, upon no weightier account than the single score of their own opinions.

FRANCIS OSBORN.

Knowledge is pleasant unto the soul.

In all labour there is profit.

Advice to a Young Tradesman.
Written in the Year 1748.

AS you have desired it of me, I write the following hints, which have been of service to me, and may, if observed, be so to you.

Remember that time is money. He that can earn ten shillings a-day by his labour, and goes abroad or sits idle one-half of that day, though he spends but sixpence during his diversion or idleness, ought not to reckon that the only expense; he has really spent, or rather thrown away, five shillings besides.

Remember that credit is money. If a man lets his money lie in my hands after it is due, he gives me the interest, or so much as I can make of it, during that time. This amounts to a considerable sum where a man has good and large credit, and makes good use of it.

Remember that money is of a prolific, generating nature. Money can beget money, and its offspring can beget more, and so on. Five shillings turned is six; turned again it is seven and threepence; and so on till it becomes a hundred pounds. The more there is of it, the more it produces every turning, so that the profits rise quicker and quicker. He that kills a breeding sow, destroys all her offspring to the thou-

He who errs in the tens errs in the thousands.

Honesty is the best policy.

Trust, but not too much.

sandth generation. He that murders a crown, destroys all that it might have produced, even scores of pounds.

Remember that six pounds a-year is but a groat a-day. For this little sum (which may be daily wasted either in time or expense, unperceived) a man of credit may, on his own security, have the constant possession and use of a hundred pounds. So much in stock, briskly turned by an industrious man, produces great advantage.

Remember this saying—" The good paymaster is lord of another man's purse." He that is known to pay punctually and exactly to the time he promises may at any time, and on any occasion, raise all the money his friends can spare. This is sometimes of great use. After industry and frugality, nothing contributes more to the raising of a young man in the world than punctuality and justice in all his dealings: therefore never keep borrowed money an hour beyond the time you promised, lest a disappointment shut up your friend's purse for ever.

The most trifling actions that affect a man's credit are to be regarded. The sound of your hammer at five in the morning, or nine at night, heard by a creditor, makes him easy six months longer; but if he sees you at a billiard-table, or hears your voice at a tavern, when you should be at work, he sends for his money the next day; demands it before he can receive it in a lump.

Order is heaven's first law.

It shows, besides, that you are mindful of what you owe; it makes you appear a careful as well as an honest man, and that still increases your credit.

Beware of thinking all your own that you possess, and of living accordingly. It is a mistake that many people who have credit fall into. To prevent this, keep an exact account, for some time, both of your expenses and your income. If you take the pains at first to mention particulars, it will have this good effect: you will discover how wonderfully small trifling expenses mount up to large sums, and will discern what might have been, and may for the future be saved, without occasioning any great inconvenience.

In short, the way to wealth, if you desire it, is as plain as the way to market. It depends chiefly on two words, *industry* and *frugality;* that is, waste neither *time* nor *money*, but make the best use of both. Without industry and frugality nothing will do, and with them everything. He that gets all he can honestly, and saves all he gets (necessary expenses excepted), will certainly become *rich*—if that Being who governs the world, to whom all should look for a blessing on their honest endeavours, doth not in his wise providence otherwise determine.

BENJAMIN FRANKLIN.

A penny saved's a penny clear;

A pin a day's a groat a year.

Time is money.

BOOKS.

IT is chiefly through books that we enjoy intercourse with superior minds; and these invaluable means of communication are within the reach of all. In the best books great men talk to us—give us their most precious thoughts, and pour their souls into ours.

God be thanked for books! They are the voices of the distant and the dead, and make us heirs of the spiritual life of past ages. Books are the true levellers. They give to all who will faithfully use them the society, the spiritual presence of the best and greatest of our race. No matter how poor I am; no matter though the prosperous of my own time will not enter my obscure dwelling. If the sacred writers will enter and take up their abode under my roof; if Milton will cross my threshold to sing to me of Paradise Lost, and Shakespeare to open to me the worlds of imagination, and the workings of the human heart, and Franklin to enrich me with his practical wisdom, I shall not pine for intellectual companionship, and I may become a cultivated man, though excluded from what is called the best society, in the place where I live.

CHANNING.

Small beginnings have great endings.

SMALL BEGINNINGS.

IT is related of Chantrey, the celebrated sculptor, that, when a boy, he was observed by a gentleman in the neighbourhood of Sheffield very attentively engaged in cutting a stick with a penknife. He asked the lad what he was doing; when, with great simplicity of manner, but with great courtesy, he replied, "I am cutting old Fox's head." Fox was the school-master of the village. On this the gentleman asked to see what he had done, and pronouncing it to be an excellent likeness, gave the youth a sixpence. And this may be reckoned the first money Chantrey ever received for the production of his art.

This anecdote is but one of a thousand that might be cited of as many different men who from small beginnings rise to stations and influence; and shows the importance of not despising the day of small things, in any condition or circumstance of life. All nature, in fact, is full of instructive lessons on this point, which it would be well for us more thoroughly to study and appreciate.

The river, rolling onward its accumulated waters to the ocean, was in its small beginning but an oozing rill, trickling down some moss-covered rock, and winding like a silver thread between the green banks to

Many littles make a mickle.

Despise not the day of small things.

Step by step climbs the hill.

By little and little the sack is filled.

which it imparted verdure. The tree that sweeps the air with its hundred branches, and mocks at the howling of the tempest, was in its small beginning but a little seed trodden under foot, unnoticed; then a small shoot that the leaping hare might have for ever crushed.

Everything around us tells us not to despise small beginnings; for they are the lower rounds of a ladder that reaches to great results, and we must step upon these before we can ascend higher.

Despise not small beginnings of wealth.

The Rothschilds, Girard, Aston, and most of the richest men began with small means. From pence they proceeded to pounds; from hundreds to thousands; and from thousands to millions. Had they neglected these first earnings, had they said within themselves, What is the use of these few coppers? they are not of much value, and I will just spend them, and enjoy myself as I go—they would never have risen to be the wealthiest among their fellows. It is only by this economical husbanding of small means that they increase to large sums. It is the hardest part of success to gain a little; this *little* once gained, *more* will easily follow.

Despise not the small beginnings of education.

Franklin had but little early education; yet look at what he became, and how he was reverenced. Ferguson, feeding his sheep on the hills of Scotland,

The ocean is made up of drops.

picked up merely the rudiments of learning, but subsequently rose to be one of the first astronomers of Europe. Herschel, the great astronomer, was in his youth a drummer-boy to a marching regiment, and received but a little more than a drummer-boy's education; but his name is now associated with the brightest discoveries of science, and is borne by the planet which his zeal discovered. A host of instances rise up to testify that, by properly improving the small and perhaps imperfect beginnings of knowledge, they may become as foundation-stones of a temple of learning, which the future shall gaze upon and admire.

A man can scarcely be too avaricious in the acquisition of knowledge; he should hoard up his intellectual gain with the utmost assiduity and diligence; but, unlike the lucre-seeking miser, must put out his knowledge at usury, and, by lending out his stock to others, increase by the commerce of his thoughts his capital, until his one talent shall have become five, and this five shall have gained to them other five.

Despise not the small beginnings of fame or honour.

The fame which springs up on a sudden, like a mushroom-plant, is seldom lasting. True fame and honour are of slow growth, ascending by degrees from the lowest offices to the highest stations—from the regard of a few to the applause of a nation. But he

Little strokes fell great oaks.

who despises the lower steps of honour, because they are low, will seldom reach the higher; and he who spurns at the commendation of his own circle, as too small a thing to seek after, will never secure the esteem and renown of a state or kingdom.

Despise not the small beginnings of error.

The walls of a castle have been undermined by the burrowings of small and despised animals; and the beginning of error, though at first unheeded, will soon, if not checked, sap the foundations of truth, and build up its own wretched dogmas on its ruins. All first errors are small; despise them not; they will soon increase to great ones, and perhaps devastate society.

MR. MICAWBER'S ADVICE.

MY advice is, never to do to-morrow what you can do to-day. "Procrastination is the thief of time." My other piece of advice is: annual income, £20; annual expenditure, £19 19s. 6d.; result, happiness. Annual income, £20; annual expenditure, £20 0s. 6d.; result, misery. The blossom is blighted, the leaf is withered, the god of day goes down upon the scene; and—in short, you are for ever floored—as I am now!"

DICKENS.

Spend less than you gain.

Small gains and often make a well-filled purse.

Half a loaf is better than no bread.

Happy is the man that findeth wisdom.

BROUGHAM'S ADVICE TO MACAULAY.

WHEN Lord Macaulay was attending college at Cambridge, Lord Brougham sent the following letter of advice to his father, Zachary Macaulay, Esq. As it contains many hints and suggestions which are as valuable at the present day as they were half a century ago, no apology is required for its introduction to our "Book of Good Devices."

"Newcastle, March 10, 1823.

"MY DEAR FRIEND,—My principal object in writing to you to-day is to offer you some suggestions, in consequence of some conversation I have just had with Lord Grey, who has spoken of your son in terms of the greatest praise. He takes his account from his son; but from all I know, and have learnt from other quarters, I doubt not that his judgment is well formed. Now you of course destine him for the bar, and assuming that this, and the public objects incidental to it, are in his views, I would fain impress upon you (and through you upon him) a truth or two which experience has made me aware of, and which I would have given a great deal to have been acquainted with earlier in life from the experience of others.

"First, That the foundation of all excellence is to be laid in early application to general knowledge is clear; that he is already aware of; and equally so it is (of which he may not be so well aware) that professional eminence can only be

Fools despise wisdom and instruction.   *Wisdom is more precious than rubies.*

Better unborn than untaught.

attained by entering betimes into the lowest drudgery, the most repulsive labours of the profession; even a year in an attorney's office, as the law is now practised, I should not hold too severe a task, or too high a price to pay, for the benefit it must surely lead to; but at all events the life of a special pleader, I am quite convinced, is the thing before being called to the bar. A young man whose mind has once been well imbued with general learning, and has acquired classical propensities, will never sink into a mere drudge. He will always save himself harmless from the dull atmosphere he must live and work in; and the sooner he will emerge from it, and arrive at eminence. But what I wish to inculcate especially, with a view to the great talent for public speaking which your son happily possesses, is that he should cultivate that talent in the only way in which it can reach the height of the art; and I wish to turn his attention to two points. I speak upon this subject with the authority both of experience and observation; I have made it very much my study in theory; have written a great deal upon it which may never see the light, and something which has been published; have meditated much, and conversed much on it with famous men; have had some little practical experience in it, but have prepared for much more than I ever tried, by a variety of laborious methods—reading, writing, much translation, composing in foreign languages, etc., and I have lived in times when there were great orators among us; therefore I reckon my opinion worth listening to, and the rather because I have the utmost confidence in it myself, and should have saved a world of trouble and much time had I started with a conviction of its truth.

"1. The first point is this: the beginning of the art is to acquire a habit of *easy speaking;* and in whatever way this can be had (which individual inclination or accident will generally direct, and may safely be allowed to do so), it must be had. Now I differ from all other doctors of rhetoric in this; I say, let him first of all learn to speak easily and fluently, as well and as sensibly as he can no doubt, but at any rate let him learn to speak. This is to eloquence, or good public speaking, what the being able to talk in a child is to correct grammatical speech. It is the requisite foundation, and on it you must build. Moreover, it can only be acquired young; therefore let it by all means, and at any sacrifice, be gotten hold of forthwith. But in acquiring it every sort of slovenly error will also be acquired. It must be got by a habit of easy writing (which, as Wyndham said, proved hard reading); by a custom of talking much in company; by speaking in debating societies, with little attention to rule, and mere love of saying something at any rate, than of saying anything well. I can even suppose that more attention is paid to the matter in such discussions than to the manner of saying it; yet still to say it easily, *ad libitum*, to be able to say what you choose, and what you have to say, this is the first requisite; to acquire which everything else must for the present be sacrificed.

"2. The next step is the grand one: to convert this style of easy speaking into chaste eloquence. And here there is but one rule. I do earnestly entreat your son to set daily and nightly before him the Greek models. First of all he may look to the best modern speeches (as he probably has already); Burke's best compositions, as the Thoughts on the Cause of the present Discontents; Speech on the American Conciliation, and On the Nabob of Arcot's Debt; Fox's Speech on the Westminster Scrutiny (the first part of which he should pore over till he has it by heart); On the Russian Armament;

Read not to contradict and confute,

and On the War, 1803; with one or two of Wyndham's best, and very few, or rather none, of Sheridan's; but he must by no means stop here; if he would be a great orator, he must go at once to the fountain-head, and be familiar with every one of the great orations of Demosthenes. I take for granted that he knows those of Cicero by heart; they are very beautiful, but not very useful, except perhaps the Milo pro Ligario, and one or two more; but the Greek must positively be the model; and merely reading it, as boys do, to know the language, won't do at all; he must enter into the spirit of each speech, thoroughly know the positions of the parties, follow each turn of the argument, and make the absolutely perfect and most chaste and severe composition familiar to his mind. His taste will improve every time he reads and repeats to himself (for he should have the fine passages by heart), and he will learn how much may be done by a skilful use of a few words, and a rigorous rejection of all superfluities. In this view I hold a familiar knowledge of Dante to be next to Demosthenes. It is in vain to say that imitations of these models won't do for our times. First, I do not counsel any imitation, but only an imbibing of the same spirit. Secondly, I know from experience that nothing is half so successful in these times (bad though they be) as what has been formed on the Greek models. I use a very poor instance in giving my own experience; but I do assure you that both in courts of law and Parliament, and even to mobs, I have never made so much play (to use a very modern phrase) as when I was almost translating from the Greek. I composed the peroration of my speech for the Queen, in the Lords, after reading and repeating Demosthenes for three or four weeks, and I composed it twenty times over at least, and it certainly succeeded in a very extraordinary degree, and far above any

Nor to find talk and discourse;

Frequent the company of your betters.

merits of its own. This leads me to remark that though speaking, with writing beforehand, is very well until the habit of easy speech is acquired, yet after that he can never write too much; this is quite clear. It is laborious, no doubt; and it is more difficult beyond comparison than speaking off-hand; but it is necessary to perfect oratory, and at any rate it is necessary to acquire the habit of correct diction. But I go further and say, even to the end of a man's life he must prepare word for word most of his finer passages. Now, would he be a great orator or no? In other words, would he have almost absolute power of doing good to mankind, in a free country, or no? So he wills this, he must follow these rules.

"Believe me truly yours,
"H. BROUGHAM."

WHAT IS DIFFICULTY?

DIFFICULTY is a severe instructor, set over us by the supreme ordinance of a parental Guardian and Legislator, who knows us better than we know ourselves, as He loves us better, too. He that wrestles with us, strengthens our nerves, and sharpens our skill: our antagonist is our helper. This amicable contest with difficulty obliges us to an intimate acquaintance with our object, and compels us to consider it in all its relations; it will not suffer us to be superficial.

BURKE.

Books are the most wholesome friends.

Mean spirits admire basely.

Learn to admire rightly.

The highest learning is to be wise,

EARL OF STRAFFORD TO HIS SON.

MY DEAREST WILL,

These are the last lines* that you are to receive from a father that tenderly loves you. I wish there were a greater leisure to impart my mind unto you; but our merciful God will supply all things by His grace, and guide and protect you in all your ways; to whose infinite goodness I bequeath you: and therefore be not discouraged, but serve Him, and trust in Him, and He will preserve and prosper you in all things.

Be sure you give all respect to my wife, that hath ever had a great love unto you, and therefore may be well becoming you. Never be wanting in your love and care to your sisters, but let them ever be most dear unto you; for this will give others cause to esteem and respect you for it, and it is a duty that you owe them in the memory of your excellent mother and myself; therefore your care and affections to them must be the very same that you are to have of yourself; and the like regard must you have to your youngest sister; for indeed you owe it her also, both for her father and mother's sake.

*The Earl of Strafford was allowed only three days between his sentence and execution. This interval he employed in writing farewell letters, settling his family affairs, and petitioning the House of Lords to show mercy to his children, to whom he was most tenderly attached.

Without counsel purposes are disappointed.

He that regardeth reproof is prudent.

The greatest wisdom is to be good.

Youth is the season God has given,

Sweet Will, be careful to take the advice of those friends which are by me desired to advise you for your education. Serve God diligently, morning and evening, and recommend yourself unto Him, and have Him before your eyes in all your ways. With patience hear the instructions of those friends I leave with you, and diligently follow their counsel; for, till you come by time to have experience in the world, it will be far more safe to trust to their judgments than your own. Lose not the time of your youth, but gather those seeds of virtue and knowledge which may be of use to yourself, and comfort to your friends, for the rest of your life. And that this may be the better effected, attend thereunto with patience, and be sure to correct and refrain yourself from anger. Suffer not sorrow to cast you down, but with cheerfulness and good courage go on the race you have to run in all sobriety and truth. Be sure, with an hallowed care, to have respect to all the commandments of God, and give not yourself to neglect them in the least things, lest by degrees you come to forget them in the greatest; for the heart of man is deceitful above all things. And in all your duties and devotions towards God, rather perform them joyfully than pensively; for God loves a cheerful giver. For your religion, let it be directed according to that which shall be taught by those who are in God's church, the proper teachers therefore, rather than that you either fancy one to

The Bible is the pole-star of eternity.

Fear the Lord, and depart from evil.

To rise from earth, and fly to heaven.

> Keep thy heart with all diligence;

yourself, or be led by men that are singular in their own opinions, and delight to go ways of their own finding out; for you will certainly find soberness and truth in the one, and much unsteadiness and vanity in the other.

The king, I trust, will deal graciously with you, and restore you those honours and that fortune which a distempered time hath deprived you of, together with the life of your father: which I rather advise might be by a new gift and creation from himself, than by any other means, to the end you may pay the thanks to him without having obligation to any other.

Be sure to avoid as much as you can to inquire after those that have been sharp in their judgments towards me; and I charge you never to suffer thought of revenge to enter your heart, but be careful to be informed who were my friends in this prosecution, and to them apply yourself to make them your friends also: and on such you may rely, and bestow much of your conversation amongst them.

And God Almighty of his infinite goodness bless you and your children's children; and His same goodness bless your sisters in like manner, perfect you in every good work, and give you right understandings in all things! Amen.

Your most loving Father.

Tower, this 11th of May, 1641.

Fear God, and honour the King.

The fear of the Lord is to hate evil.

> For out of it are the issues of life.

One To-day is worth two To-morrows.

You must not fail to behave yourself towards my Lady Clare, your grandmother, with all duty and observance; for most tenderly doth she love you, and hath been passing kind unto me; God reward her charity for it. And both in this and all the rest, the same that I counsel you, the same do I direct also to your sisters, that so the same may be observed by you all. And once more do I, from my very soul, beseech our gracious God to bless and govern you in all, to the saving you in the day of His visitation, and join us again in the communion of His blessed saints, where is fulness of joy and bliss for evermore. Amen. Amen.

TO-MORROW.

TO-MORROW you will live, you always cry.
In what far country does this morrow lie,
That 'tis so mighty long ere it arrive?
Beyond the Indies does this morrow live?
'Tis so far-fetch'd, this morrow, that I fear
'Twill be both very old and very dear.
"To-morrow I will live," the fool doth say;
To-day itself, too late; the wise lived yesterday!

To-morrow is the fool's holiday.

Procrastination is the thief of time.

By the street of By-and-by, we arrive at the house of Never.

SEVEN THINGS GOD HATES.

"Six things doth the Lord hate; yea, seven are an abomination unto him."—PROV. vi. 16.

I. Haughtiness, conceitedness of ourselves, and contempt of others; *a proud look*. There are seven things that God hates, and pride is the first, because it is at the bottom of much sin, and gives rise to it. God sees the pride in the heart, and hates it there; but when it prevails to that degree, that the show of men's countenance witnesses against them, that they over-value themselves, and under-value all about them, this is in a special manner hateful to Him; for there pride is proud of itself, and sets shame at defiance.

II. Falsehood, and fraud, and dissimulation. Next to a proud look, nothing is more an abomination to God than a *lying tongue*; nothing more sacred than truth, nor more necessary to conversation than speaking truth; God and all good men hate and abhor lying.

III. Cruelty and blood-thirstiness. The devil was, from the beginning, a liar and a murderer, and therefore as a lying tongue, so *hands that shed innocent blood* are hateful to God, because they have in them the devil's image, and do him service.

IV. Subtlety in the contrivance of sin, wisdom to do evil, *a heart that* designs, and a head that *devises wicked imaginations*, that is acquainted with the depths of Satan, and knows how to carry on a covetous, envious, revengeful plot most effectually. The more there is of craft and management in sin, the more it is an abomination to God.

V. Vigour and diligence in the prosecution of sin; *feet that are swift in running to mischief*, as if they were afraid of losing time, or were impatient of delay, in a thing they are so greedy of. The policy and vigilance, the eagerness and industry, of sinners in their sinful pursuits, may shame us who go about that which is good so awkwardly and so coldly.

VI. *False-witness bearing*, which is one of the greatest mischiefs that the wicked imagination can devise, and against which there is least fence. There cannot be a greater affront to God, to whom in an oath appeal is made, or a greater injury to our neighbour, all whose interests in this world, even the dearest, lie open to an attack of this kind, than knowingly to give in a false testimony. There are seven things that God hates, and lying involves two of them; He hates it and doubly hates it.

VII. Making mischief between relations and neighbours, and using all wicked means possible, not only to alienate their affections one from another, but to irritate their passions one against another. The God of love and peace hates *him that sows discord among brethren*, for He delights in concord. Those that, by

Evil words cut more than swords.

tale-bearing and slandering, by carrying ill-natured stories, aggravating everything that is said and done, and suggesting jealousies and evil surmises, blow the coals of contention, are but preparing for themselves a fire of the same nature.

MATTHEW HENRY.

PAYING DEBTS.

WHAT pleasure it is to pay one's debts! I remember to have heard Sir Thomas Lyttleton make this observation. It seems to flow from a combination of circumstances, each of which is productive of pleasure. In the first place, it removes that uneasiness which a true spirit feels from dependence and obligation. It affords pleasure to the creditor, and therefore gratifies our social affection. It promotes that future confidence which is so very interesting to an honest mind. It opens a prospect of being readily supplied with what we want on future occasions. It leaves a consciousness of our own virtue; and it is a measure we know to be right, both in point of justice and sound economy. Finally, it is the main support of simple reputation.

SHENSTONE.

Get and save, and thou wilt have.

He is rich that hath no debt.

Debt means danger.

Duty never yet did want its meed.

Collingwood's Advice.

ADMIRAL COLLINGWOOD was an ardent devotee of duty. "Do your duty to the best of your ability," was the maxim which he urged upon young men when setting out in life. To a midshipman he on one occasion gave the following manly and sensible advice:—

You may depend upon it, that it is more in your own power than in anybody else's to promote both your comfort and advancement. A strict and unwearied attention to your duty, and a complacent and respectful behaviour, not only to your superiors but to everybody, will ensure you their regard, and the reward will surely come; but if it should not, I am convinced you have too much good sense to let disappointment sour you. Guard carefully against letting discontent appear in you. It will be sorrow to your friends, a triumph to your competitors, and cannot be productive of any good. Conduct yourself so as to deserve the best that can come to you, and the consciousness of your own proper behaviour will keep you in spirits if it should not come. Let it be your ambition to be foremost in all duty. Do not be a nice observer of turns, but ever present yourself ready for everything, and, unless your officers are very inattentive men, they will not allow others to impose more duty on you than they should.

Attention to superiors is a duty.

Do your duty, come what will.

All difficulties are but easy when they are known.

The Pursuit of Wealth.

IT is not surprising that our young men become easily inflamed with an inordinate desire for property. They see its power in the world; that wealth can hire the strong, retain the learned, and secure honour, or at least place, in society. Hence pride seeks money, to give it elevation; vanity seeks it, to attract the admiration and excite the envy of others; and avarice seeks it, to fall down and worship it.

Money itself is good—in the words of Solomon, "it answereth all things;" not only luxury, but comfort, convenience, necessity demand it. And yet the acquisition of it is beset with moral perils. In our insane eagerness to be rich, we delude ourselves with the idea that gold can fill and satisfy the soul. We regard no calamity so great as pecuniary want. The boy has his money-box, and learns to hoard as he learns to speak. "The chief end of man," he is taught, is to make a good bargain. He is fired with a passion to set up in business for himself prematurely, and to rush into every path that seems to open out into a boundless accumulation of wealth.

Two tempters stand before the young man, and beckon him to follow them. First, a reckless speculation. Under this influence, men are ready to invest their all in projects, the greater portion of which are chimerical. Bales of goods and risks of commissions are staked at the table; and even many kinds of business, once followed with honesty, moderation, and a healthy success, are now pursued as games of chance. Not a few merchants thus spread out their business till it gets beyond their control; they overbuy goods; they live beyond their means, trusting that at last everything will come right. So eager are they for all possible investments that, as one said, "If it were proposed to build a bridge to Tophet, the shares would readily be taken up." But soon every mercantile project so founded totters to its fall, and great is the fall thereof.

Others, in their passion for sudden accumulation, practise secret frauds, and imagine that there is no harm in them, so long as they are undetected. But in vain will they cover up their transgression, for God sees it to the very bottom; and let them not hope to keep it always from man.

In the long web of events, "be sure your sin will find you out." He who is carrying on a course of latent corruption and dishonesty—be he engaged in some mammoth speculation, or involved only in lesser private transactions—is sailing in a ship like that fabled one of old, which comes ever nearer and nearer to a magnetic mountain, that will at last draw every nail out of it, and scatter its timbers to the waves. Faith in God and all trust in man will eventually be lost, and he will get no reward for his guilt. The winds will sigh forth his iniquity; and "a beam will come out of the wall," to convict and smite him.

Better the noble resolution of Franklin — "My years roll round," said he, writing to his honoured mother, in early manhood, "and the last will come, when I had rather have it said, 'he lived usefully,' than that 'he died rich.'"

BORROWING.

BEWARE of suretyship for thy best friend. He that payeth another man's debt, seeketh his own decay. But if thou canst not otherwise choose, rather lend thy money thyself upon good bonds, although thou borrow it. So shalt thou secure thyself, and pleasure thy friend. Neither borrow money of a neighbour or a friend, but of a stranger; where, paying for it, thou shalt hear no more of it. Otherwise thou shalt eclipse thy credit, lose thy freedom, and yet pay as dear as to another. But in borrowing of money be precious of thy word; for he that hath care of keeping days of payment is lord of another man's purse.

LORD BURLEIGH.

The use of knowledge is to know God.

THE USE OF KNOWLEDGE.

OF knowledge, as of wealth, the true value depends upon its use. Laid up, under lock and key, in the coffers of the miser, the largest amount of riches, in bags of rusting gold and silver, serves no good end. Its owner may please himself with the thought of having it, and of being known to have it. He may take delight in opening his chests and gloating his eyes from time to time on his accumulating heaps; but how mean and pitiful such a gratification even to a reasonable, and how much more to a morally responsible being! Yet, in a similar way, a man may plume himself on the extent and variety of his knowledge. He may feed his vanity in enumerating to himself its subjects, and the amount of it on each. And the gratification arising from the possession of it—apart from the thoughts of vanity—may be of a far higher and more rational kind than that of the former; but if its possessor keeps it all hidden in the depths of his own mind—shut up in the coffers of his memory, uncommunicated, unapplied to any useful purpose—what character does he bear but that of being an intellectual miser?

DR. WARDLAW.

Understanding is a well-spring of life unto him that hath it.

Knowledge is the candle by which Faith sees to work.

All our knowledge is, ourselves to know.

Righteousness exalteth a nation.

Precepts of Gold.

STRIVE not with a mighty man, lest thou fall into his hands.

Be not at variance with a rich man, lest he overweigh thee: for gold hath destroyed many, and perverted the hearts of kings.

Strive not with a man that is full of tongue, and heap not tongue upon his fire.

Jest not with a rude man, lest thy ancestors be disgraced.

Reproach not a man that turneth from sin; but remember that we are all worthy of punishment.

Dishonour not a man in his old age; for even some of us wax old.

Rejoice not over thy greatest enemy being dead, but remember that we die all.

Despise not the discourse of the wise, but acquaint thyself with their proverbs; for of them thou shalt learn instruction, and how to serve great men with ease.

Miss not the discourse of the elders; for they also learned of their fathers, and of them thou shalt learn understanding, and to give answer as need requireth.

ECCLESIASTICUS.

Sin is a reproach to any people.

By the fear of the Lord men depart from evil.

A mind content both crown and kingdom is.

Hopes and fears checker human life.

POLONIUS TO LAERTES.

THESE few precepts in thy memory.
   See thou character. Give thy thoughts no
     tongue,
   Nor any unproportioned thought his act.
   Be thou familiar, but by no means vulgar.
   Those friends thou hast, and their adoption tried,
Grapple them to thy soul with hoops of steel;
But do not dull thy palm with entertainment
Of each new-hatch'd, unfledged comrade. Beware
Of entrance to a quarrel, but being in,
Bear't that the opposed may beware of thee.
Give every man thy ear, but few thy voice;
Take each man's censure, but reserve thy judgment.
Costly thy habit as thy purse can buy,
But not express'd in fancy; rich, not gaudy;
For the apparel oft proclaims the man,
And they in France of the best rank and station,
Are of a most select and generous chief in that.
Neither a borrower nor a lender be;
For loan oft loses both itself and friend,
And borrowing dulls the edge of husbandry.
This above all: to thine ownself be true,
And it must follow, as the night the day,
Thou canst not then be false to any man.
                         SHAKESPEARE.

Thrice is he armed that hath his quarrel just.

Suspicion always haunts the guilty mind.

Anger is no attribute of justice.

By doing nothing, we do ill.

NOTHING TO DO.

THERE are few words from the lips of a youth that furnish so broad an invitation to the tempter as those too frequent ones, "I have nothing to do." They form the motto with which many a besotted wretch has set out on his downward career, and might be inscribed as the epitaph upon the grave of the degraded drunkard, the infatuated gambler, the slave of lust and sensuality, and the high-handed criminal.

"Nothing to do!" What, with that immortal mind to be trained and informed with truth and wisdom; with those exalted powers within you, for whose improvement you are so soon to give account; with those hands that are so strong for toil; with that soul that shall live or die for ever?

"Nothing to do!" Oh, say it not when thy brother is perishing; when desolate hearts are waiting your kind mission to them; when there are burdens to be lifted from the weary, and tears to be wiped from the eye of sorrow!

Be not a drone in God's busy hive; the world, in these stirring days, has no room for such; but make haste to fill your minds, your hands, with blessed activities, that they may be proportionably emptied of sin and sorrow.

A slothful hand makes a slim fortune.

If Satan find you idle, he'll set you to work.

Idle young, needy old.

DELAYS.

HUN delays, they breed remorse;
  Take thy time while time is lent thee;
Creeping snails have weakest force,
  Fly their fault, lest thou repent thee;
    Good is best when sooner wrought,
    Ling'ring labours come to nought.

Hoist up sail while gale doth last,
  Tide and wind stay no man's pleasure!
Seek not time when time is past,
  Sober speed is wisdom's leisure;
    After-wits are dearly bought,
    Let thy fore-wit guide thy thought.

Time wears all his locks before,
  Take thou hold upon his forehead;
When he flees he turns no more,
  And behind his scalp is naked.
    Works adjourn'd have many stays,
    Long demurs breed new delays.
                  SOUTHWELL.

A working hand is worth gold.

OVERCOME DIFFICULTIES.

THERE are few difficulties that hold out against real attacks: they fly, like the visible horizon, before those who advance. A passionate desire and unwearied will can perform impossibilities, or what seem to be such to the cold and the feeble. If we do but go on, some unseen path will open upon the hills. We must not allow ourselves to be discouraged by the apparent disproportion between the result of single efforts, and the magnitude of the obstacles to be encountered. Nothing good or great is to be obtained without courage and industry; but courage and industry might have sunk in despair, and the world must have remained unornamented and unimproved, if men had nicely compared the effect of a single stroke of the chisel with the pyramid to be raised, or of a single impression of the spade with the mountain to be levelled. All exertion, too, is in itself delightful, and active amusements seldom tire us. Helvetius owns that he could hardly listen to a concert for two hours, though he could play on an instrument all day long. The chase, we know, has always been the favourite amusement of kings and nobles. Not only fame and fortune, but pleasure is

Courage is the salt of life.

Industrious youth makes easy age.

to be earned. Efforts, it must not be forgotten, are as indispensable as desires. The globe is not to be circumnavigated by one wind. We should never do nothing. "It is better to wear out than to rust out," says Bishop Cumberland. "There will be time enough for repose in the grave," said Nicole to Pascal. In truth, the proper rest for man is change of occupation. As a young man, you should be mindful of the unspeakable importance of early industry, since in youth habits are easily formed, and there is time to recover from defects. An Italian sonnet, justly as well as elegantly, compares procrastination to the folly of a traveller who pursues a brook till it widens into a river and is lost in the sea. The toils as well as risks of an active life are commonly overrated, so much may be done by the diligent use of ordinary opportunities; but they must not always be waited for. We must not only strike the iron while it is hot, but till "it is made hot." Herschel, the great astronomer, declares that ninety or a hundred hours clear enough for observations cannot be called an unproductive year. The lazy, the dissipated, and the fearful should not patiently see the active and the bold pass them in the course. Those who have not energy to work must learn to be humble, and should not vainly hope to unite the incompatible enjoyments of indolence and enterprise, of ambition and self-indulgence.

Better wear out than rust out.

Wisdom's ways are ways of pleasantness,

THE USE OF LEISURE.

I CONGRATULATE you upon the increasing attention which is evidently paid to the objects of sensible science. By the studies of natural history, my young friends, you become acquainted with "the wondrous works of HIM that is excellent in knowledge," and, by those of natural philosophy, you investigate the causes and results of the changes which you or others have observed in the objects noticed by your senses. This is a part at least of what the wise man describes as "applying the heart to know, and to search, and to seek out wisdom and the reason of things." . . . It is one of our blessings, by God's kind providence, to live in a time when literature, science, and the arts are cultivated so assiduously, and their results are proclaimed so widely, that the necessity of acquiring general knowledge is strongly impressed, and the means of the acquisition are afforded with unexampled facility. To many, however, the measure of such acquisition must be imperfect. The indispensable cares and labours of our earthly condition present insurmountable obstacles; and there are duties of personal religion and of social life which possess an infinitely higher obligation, and the neglect of which would bring guilt upon our

And all her paths are peace.

As you sow, so must you reap.

consciences, and injury upon our dearest connections. . . . Some are privileged to enjoy a good measure of evening hours: let them not neglect the gift which the benignity of Providence thus confers upon them. Their leisure is a talent too precious, and its responsibility is a weight too awful to be treated lightly. The cultivation of natural history and the sciences will be dignified means of excluding those modes of abusing time, which are the sin and disgrace of many young persons—vapid indolence, frivolous conversation, amusements which bring no good fruit to the mind or the heart, or such reading as only feasts the imagination while it enervates the judgment and diminishes or annihilates the faculty of command over the thoughts and affections; a faculty whose healthy exercise is essential to real dignity of character. . . . But there are many of the most estimable men who cannot enjoy this advantage. Yet let them not be discouraged. Let them take increasing pains (according to their opportunities, and without infringing upon the requisite degree of physical exercise) to cultivate the habit of close observation and exact attention. Let them make up by repetition what they lack in continuity. Small portions of time, linked together by constancy of return and closeness of succession, will form, in months and years, a noble amount of improvement.

JOHN PYE SMITH, D.D.

Prove all things; hold fast that which is good.

He that walketh uprightly, walketh surely.

Wise men lay up knowledge.

Be strong in the Lord.

THE FRUITS OF A FATHER'S LOVE.

MY DEAR CHILDREN,

THESE are the gifts and mercies of the God of your tender father. Hear my counsel, and lay it up in your hearts. Love it more than treasure, and follow it, and you shall be blessed here, and happy hereafter.

In the first place, remember your Creator in the days of your youth. It was the glory of Israel; and how did God bless Josiah because he feared Him in his youth! and so He did Jacob, Joseph, and Moses. To do this in your youthful days, seek after the Lord that you may find Him; remembering His great love in creating you; that you are not beasts, plants, or stones, but that He has kept you, and given you His grace within and substance without, and provided plentifully for you. This remember in your youth, that you may be kept from the evil of the world; for in age it will be harder to overcome the temptations of it.

Wherefore, my dear children, eschew the appearance of evil, and love and cleave to that in your hearts which shows you evil from good, and tells you when you do amiss, and reproves you for it. It is the light of Christ that He has given you for your salvation. If you do this, and follow my counsel,

Learn to do well.

Evil principles lead to evil practices.

Be not rash with thy mouth.

Choose not alone a proper mate,

God will bless you in this world, and give you an inheritance in that which shall never have an end.

Next, be obedient to your dear mother—a woman whose virtue and good name is an honour to you; for she hath been exceeded by none in her time for her plainness, integrity, industry, humanity, virtue, and good understanding; qualities not usual among women of her worldly condition and quality. Therefore honour and obey her, my dear children, as your mother, and your father's love and delight; nay, love her too, for she loved your father with a deep and upright love, choosing him before all her other many suitors. . . I charge you before the Lord, honour and obey, love and cherish your dear mother.

Next, betake yourselves to some honest, industrious course of life, and that not of sordid covetousness, but for example and to avoid idleness. And if you change your condition and marry, choose with the knowledge and consent of your mother if living, or of guardians, or those that have the charge of you. Mind neither beauty or riches, but the fear of the Lord, and a sweet and amiable disposition, such as you can love above all this world, and that may make your habitations pleasant and desirable to you. Live in the fear of the Lord, and He will bless you and your offspring. Be sure to live within compass; borrow not, neither be beholden to any. Ruin not yourselves by kindness to others, for that exceeds the

But proper time to marry.

The way of the just is uprightesness.

The lips of the righteous feed many.

A grateful mind is a great mind.

due bounds of friendship—neither will a true friend expect it. Let your industry and parsimony go no further than for a sufficiency for life, and to make a provision for your children, and that in moderation, if the Lord gives you any. I charge you help the poor and needy; let the Lord have a voluntary share of your income for the good of the poor, for we are all His creatures; remembering that "he that giveth to the poor lendeth to the Lord."

Know well your in-comings, and your out-goings may be better regulated. Love not money nor the world; use them only, and they will serve you; but if you love them you serve them, which will debase your spirits as well as offend the Lord.

Pity the distressed, and hold out a hand of help to them; it may be your case; and as you mete to others, God will mete to you again.

Be humble and gentle in your conversation; of few words, I charge you, but always pertinent when you speak, hearing out before you attempt to answer, and then speaking as if you would persuade, not impose.

Affront none, neither revenge the affronts done to you; but forgive, and you shall be forgiven by your Heavenly Father.

In making friends, consider well first; and when you are fixed be true, not wavering by reports nor deserting affliction, for that becomes not the good and virtuous.

Love covereth all sins.

Be temperate in all things.

Watch against anger, neither speak nor act in it; for, like drunkenness, it makes a man a beast, and throws people into desperate inconveniences.

Avoid flatterers, for they are thieves in disguise; their praise is costly, designing to get by those they bespeak; they are the worst of creatures—they lie to flatter, and flatter to cheat; and, which is worse, if you believe them you cheat yourself most dangerously. But the virtuous, though poor, love, cherish, and prefer. Remember David, who asking the Lord, "Who shall abide in thy tabernacle? who shall dwell upon thy holy hill?" answers, "He that walketh uprightly, worketh uprighteousness, and speaketh the truth in his heart; in whose eyes the vile person is contemned, but honoureth them who fear the Lord."

Next, my children, be temperate in all things; in your diet, for that is physic by prevention—it keeps, nay, it makes people healthy, and their generation sound. This is exclusive of the spiritual advantage it brings. Be also plain in your apparel; keep out that lust which reigns too much over some; let your virtues be your ornaments, remembering life is more than food, and the body more than raiment. Let your furniture be simple and cheap. Avoid price, avarice, and luxury. Make your conversation with the most eminent for wisdom and piety; and shun all wicked men as you hope for the blessing of God, and the comfort of your father's living and

The heart of the wicked is little worth.

Speak not evil of any man.

dying prayers. Be sure you speak no evil of any, no, not of the meanest; much less of your superiors, as magistrates, guardians, tutors, teachers, and elders in Christ.

Be no busybodies; meddle not with other folk's matters, but when in conscience and duty pressed, for it procures trouble, and is ill manners, and very unseemly to wise men.

In your families remember Abraham, Moses, and Joshua, their integrity to the Lord; and do as you have them for examples.

Let the fear and service of the Living God be encouraged in your houses, and that plainness, sobriety, and moderation in all things as becometh God's chosen people; and as I advise you, my dear children, do you counsel yours if God should give you any. Yea, I counsel and command them as my posterity, that they love and serve the Lord God with an upright heart, that He may bless you and yours from generation to generation.

And as for you, who are likely to be concerned in the government of Pennsylvania, and my parts of East Jersey, especially the first, I do charge you before the Lord God and His holy angels, that you be lowly, diligent, and tender, fearing God, loving the people, and hating covetousness. Let justice have its impartial course, and the law free passage. Though to your loss, protect no man against it; for you are

It is not enough to speak, but to speak true.

Truth hath better deeds, than words, to grace it.

All pride is willing pride.

Be not afraid of sudden fear.

not above the law, but the law above you. Live therefore the lives yourselves you would have the people live, and then you have right and boldness to punish the transgressor. Keep upon the square, for God sees you; therefore do your duty, and be sure you see with your own eyes, and hear with your own ears. Entertain no lurchers, cherish no informers for gain or revenge; use no tricks; fly to no devices to support or cover injustice; but let your hearts be upright before God, trusting in Him above the contrivances of men, and none shall be able to hurt or supplant.

Oh! the Lord is a strong God, and he can do whatever he pleases; and though men consider it not, it is the Lord that rules and over-rules in the kingdoms of men, and He builds up and pulls down. I, your father, am the man that can say, "He that trusts in the Lord shall not be confounded."

Finally, my children, love one another with a true endeared love, and your dear relations on both sides, and take care to preserve tender affection in your children to each other. . . . . .

So farewell to my thrice dearly-beloved wife and children!

Yours, as God pleaseth, in that which no waters can quench, no time forget, nor distance wear away, but remains for ever, WILLIAM PENN.

Worminghurst, fourth of sixth month, 1682.

The tongue of the just is as choice silver.

Withhold not good from them to whom it is due.

The path of the just is as a shining light.

Well begun is half done.

ACTIVITY NOT ALWAYS ENERGY.

THERE are some men whose failure to succeed in life is a problem to others, as well as to themselves. They are industrious, prudent, and economical; yet, after a long life of striving, old age finds them still poor. They complain of ill-luck; they say fate is against them. But the real truth is that their projects miscarry because they mistake mere activity for energy. Confounding two things essentially different, they suppose that if they are always busy, they must of a necessity be advancing their fortune; forgetting that labour misdirected is but a waste of activity.

The person who would succeed in life is like a marksman firing at a target—if his shot misses the mark, it is but a waste of powder; to be of any service at all, it must tell in the bull's-eye or near it. So, in the great game of life, what a man does must be made to count, or it had almost as well be left undone.

The idle warrior, cut from a block of wood, who fights the air on the top of a weather-cock, instead of being made to turn some machine commensurate with his strength, is not more worthless than the merely active man who, though busy from sunrise to sunset, dissipates his labour on trifles, when he ought skilfully to concentrate it on some great end.

Duties cannot have too much diligence.

Boast not thyself of to-morrow.

Some look up, others look down.

Never venture, never win.

Every person knows some one in his circle of acquaintance who, though always active, has this want of energy. The distemper, if we may call it such, exhibits itself in various ways. In some cases, the man has merely an executive faculty when he should have a directing one; in other words, he makes a capital clerk for himself, when he ought to do the thinking work of his establishment. In other cases, what is done is either not done at the right time, or in the right way. Sometimes there is no distinction made between objects of different magnitudes, and as much labour is bestowed on a trivial affair as on a matter of great moment.

Energy, correctly understood, is activity proportioned to the end. The first Napoleon would often, when in a campaign, remain for days without undressing himself, now galloping from point to point, now dictating despatches, now studying maps and directing operations. But his periods of repose, when the crisis was over, were generally as protracted as his previous exertions had been. He has been known to sleep for eighteen hours without waking. Second-rate men, slaves of tape and routine, while they would fall short of the superhuman exertions of the great emperor, would have considered themselves lost beyond hope if they imitated what they call his indolence. They are capital illustrations of activity, keeping up their monotonous jog-trot for ever; while

Look before you leap.

Do well and have well.

Napoleon, with his gigantic industry, alternating with such apparent idleness, is an example of energy.

We do not mean to imply that chronic indolence, if relieved occasionally by spasmodic fits of industry, is to be recommended. Men who have this character run into the opposite extreme of that which we have been stigmatising, and fail as invariably of securing success in life. To call their occasional periods of application energy, would be a sad misnomer. Such persons, indeed, are but civilised savages, so to speak; vagabonds at heart in their secret hatred of work, and only resorting to labour occasionally, like the wild Indian who, after lying for weeks about his hut, is roused by sheer hunger to start on a hunting excursion. Real energy is persevering, steady, disciplined. It never either loses sight of the object to be accomplished, nor intermits its exertions while there is a possibility of success. Napoleon on the plains of Champagne, sometimes fighting two battles in one day, first defeating the Russians and then turning on the Austrians, is an illustration of this energy. The Duke of Brunswick, idling away precious time when he invaded France at the outbreak of the first Revolution, is an example to the contrary. Activity beats about a cover like an untrained dog, never lighting on the covey. Energy goes straight to the bird at once and captures it.

FREEMAN HUNT.

A wise man changes his opinion—the fool never.

Every way of a man is right in his own eyes.

Well is that well is.

Perseverance overcometh difficulties.

The Ladder of Life.

THE steps from the bottom of the ladder of fortune to the summit are not many, nor, after a knowledge of what they are constituted has been acquired, are they difficult to ascend. Each has a name and a nature which must be distinctly learned and understood by all who would seek to climb. The first step is faith, and without this none can safely rise; the second, industry; the third, perseverance; the fourth, temperance; the fifth, probity; and the sixth, independence. Having gained this position on the ladder, the future rise is easy; for faith will have taught the climber never to doubt or despair; industry will have kept him from vice, either in thought or deed; perseverance will have shown him how easily difficulties are surmounted when calmly met; temperance will have preserved both health and temper; probity will have ensured respect and given stability to the character; and independence of spirit, while it gives dignity to the man, will also gain the admiration of the world. One step more has to be acquired, which is experience, the only true knowledge of life, and then the summit of the ladder is within easy reach.

Eagles fly alone, but sheep herd together.

The word of an honest man's enough.

Acquire and beget a temperance.

Earl Strafford to Sir William Saville.

LIVE in your own house; order and understand your own estate; inform and employ yourself in the affairs of the country; carry yourself respectfully and kindly towards your neighbours; desire the company of such as are well governed and discreet amongst them, and make them as much as you can your friends; in country business keeping yourself from all faction; and at the first be not too positive, or take too much upon you, till you fully understand the course of proceedings; for, have but a little patience, and the command and government of that part of the country will infallibly fall into your hands, with honour to yourself and contentment to others; whereas, if you catch at it too soon, it will be but a means to publish your want of understanding and modesty, and that you shall grow cheap and in contempt before them that shall see you undertake that, where you are not able to guide yourself in your own way.

Be sure to moderate your expense, so as it may be without foolish waste or mean savings; take your own accounts, and betimes inure yourself to examine how your estate prospers, where it suffers, or where it may be improved; otherwise there will such an

Look not upon the wine when it is red.

easiness and neglect gather upon you, as it may be you will never patiently endure the labour of it whilst you live, and so, as much as in you lies, cast from you that which tends most to the preservation of your fortune of any other thing; for I am persuaded few men that understood their expense ever wasted; and few that do not ever well govern their estate. . .

For your servants, neither use them so familiarly as to lose your reverence at their hands, nor so disdainfully as to purchase yourself their ill-will; but carry it in an equal temper towards them, both in punishments and rewards. . . .

Let no company or respect ever draw you to excess in drink, for be you well assured that if ever that possess you, you are instantly drunk to all honour and employments in the State; drunk to all the respects your friends will otherwise pay you, and shall by unequal staggering paces go to your grave with confusion of face, as well in them that love you as in yourself. Therefore abhor all company that might entice you that way.

Spend not too much time, nor venture too much money, at gaming; it is a great vanity that possesseth some men, and in most is occasioned by a greedy mind of winning, which is a pursuit not becoming a generous noble heart, which will not brook such starving considerations as those.

In a word, guide yourself in all things in the paths

Reprove not a scorner, lest he hate thee.

To be courteous to inferiors is a duty.

The Lord is good to all.

Idleness is the parent of crime.

of goodness and virtue, and so persevere therein that you may thence take out those rules which, being learnt, may, when it comes to your turn, as well grace and enable you to lead and govern others as, whilst you are learning of them, it will become you to follow and obey others; and thus shall you possess your youth in modesty, and your elder years in wisdom.

God Almighty prosper and bless you, in your person, in your lady, in your children, and in your estate, wherein no friend you have shall take more contentment than your most affectionate uncle and most faithful friend,

STRAFFORD.

Dublin Castle, this 29th of December, 1633.

IDLENESS.

THE most concealed, and yet the most violent of all our passions, is usually that of idleness. It lays adamantine chains of death and of darkness upon us. It holds in chains, that cannot be shaken off, all our other inclinations, however tempestuous. That no more mischief is done in the world, is very much owing to a spontaneous lassitude on the minds of men, as well as that no more good is done.

An idle brain is the devil's workshop.

Laziness shall cover a man with rags.

The devil's an enemy to mankind.

Fools die for want of wisdom.

Advice to a Reckless Youth.

LEARN to be wise, and practise how to thrive,
  That would I have you do; and not to spend
  Your coin on every bauble that you fancy,
Or every foolish brain that humours you.
I would not have you to invade each place,
Nor thrust yourself on all societies,
Till men's affections, or your own desert,
Should worthily invite you to your rank.
He that is so respectless in his courses,
Oft sells his reputation at cheap market.
Nor would I you should melt away yourself
In flashing bravery, lest, while you affect
To make a blaze of gentry to the world,
A little puff of scorn extinguish it,
And you be left like an unsavoury snuff,
Whose property is only to offend.
I'd ha' you sober, and contain yourself;
Not that your sail be bigger than your boat;
But moderate your expenses now (at first),
As you may keep the same proportion still.
Nor stand so much on your gentility,
Which is an airy and mere borrow'd thing
From dead men's dust and bones, and none of yours,
Except you make, or hold it.

                        BEN JONSON.

Fools despise wisdom and instruction.

Words without thoughts never to heaven go.

Evil shall slay the wicked.

He is worth gold who can win it.

INDUSTRY.

INDUSTRY is the basis of reputation and credit. "The sound of your hammer at five in the morning, or nine at night," said Benjamin Franklin, "heard by a creditor, will make him easy six months longer; but if he sees you at a billiard-table, or hears your voice at a tavern, when you should be at your work, he sends for his money the next day." Industry is the best preventive of vice. The moment we are unemployed, the evil spirit begins to whisper to us some temptation.

"Idleness," says a quaint old author, "is the broom that sweepeth clean all good thoughts out of the house of the mind, making it fit to receive the seven devils." It is the vicious idler who robs and murders, that he may get gain; it is the merry idler who resorts to the cards and to the dice-box; it is the sensual idler who lurks for purity to defile.

Industry is often a substitute for great abilities. "Labour, well directed, is better than mere talent," said a late judge. No man is doing more to advance the great interests of education, temperance, and good morals in general, than he who promotes the industry of the community by working steadily himself, and furnishing others a regular occupation.

Industry is the parent of independence.

Industry breaks ill fortune.

A working hand is worth gold..

Find a way or make one.

A life of idleness is, usually, a life of sin; it is at best a life of utter uselessness. In the parable of the sheep and the goats, the king condemns those on the left hand for their indolence, because they have not done good to the sick and the needy.

It is surprising how much one will accomplish simply by beginning life with a steady, unremitting energy. "In looking back on my youth," says Hugh Miller, "I see that a right use of the opportunities of instruction afforded me in early youth would have made me a scholar ere my twentieth year, and have saved me at least ten years of my life."

Industry is the parent of independence. He who never stops to ask, "Why will not some one help me?" but sets out and helps himself, cannot fail of success. It is not seldom those who idly lean upon others that complain most of bad fortune. He who has a single object before him, and keeps to it, is not a man who whines about ill-success. If a youth is indolent and vacillating; if he stands waiting for something to turn up in his favour; if he loiters about, telling us he sees no opening, he should not expect success. Let him adopt the old Roman maxim: "Either I will find a way, or make one." If no good opportunity presents itself, let him resolve to make one for himself. If he cannot obtain the highest position he desires, let him take the next best that he can get. Anything is better than idleness. It is amazing what results flow

Make a spoon or spoil a horn.

from the simplest means, when adhered to resolutely. A farmer who had a noble band of sons, was asked how he managed to make them all do so well. His brief and blunt reply was, "I make them go to bed tired."

NEVER DESPAIR.

THE salt of character is a good courage. Some, because they have once or twice met with rebuffs, sink in discouragement. Such should know that our own errors may often teach us more than the grave precepts of others.

Let us counsel the young man never to despair. If he can make nothing by any work that presents itself now, he can at least make himself; or, what is equivalent, he can save himself from the sure death of a pusillanimous, halting, irresolute spirit.

Never be cast down by misfortunes. If a spider break his web, over and over he will mend it again. And do not you fall behind the very insect on your walls. If the sun is going down, look up to the stars; if earth is dark, keep your eye on heaven. With the presence and promise of God, we can bear up under anything; and should press on, and never falter or fear.

Against Idleness.

IDLENESS is the bane of body and mind, the nurse of naughtiness, the chief mother of all mischief, one of the seven deadly sins, the devil's cushion, his pillow and chief reposal. . . . . An idle dog will be mangy; and how shall an idle person escape? Idleness of the mind is much worse than that of the body; wit, without employment, is a disease—the rust of the soul, a plague, a hell itself. As in a standing pool worms and filthy creepers increase, so do evil and corrupt thoughts in an idle person; the soul is contaminated. . . . . Thus much I dare boldly say: he or she that is idle, be they of what condition they will, never so rich, so well allied, fortunate, happy—let them have all things in abundance and felicity that heart can wish and desire, all contentment—so long as he, or she, or they are idle, they shall never be pleased, never well in body or mind, but weary still, sickly still, vexed still, loathing still, weeping, sighing, grieving, suspecting, offended with the world, with every object, wishing themselves gone or dead, or else carried away with some foolish phantasy or other.

BURTON.

Fame is not gained on a feather bed.

VARIOUS WAYS OF GETTING ON.

THERE are different ways of "getting on," as progress is sometimes called in this world. It does not always mean making a large sum of money, or being a great man for people to look up at with wonder. Leaving off a bad habit for a good one is getting on; to be clean and tidy, instead of dirty and disorderly, is getting on; to be careful and saving, instead of thoughtless and extravagant, is getting on; to be active and industrious, instead of idle and lazy, is getting on; to be kind and forbearing, instead of ill-natured and quarrelsome, is getting on; to work as diligently in the master's absence as in his presence, is getting on; in short, when we see any one properly attentive to his duties, persevering through difficulties, to gain such knowledge as shall be of use to himself and others, offering a good example to his relatives and acquaintances, we may be sure that he is getting on in the world. Money is a very useful article in its way, but it is possible to get on with but small means; for it is a mistake to suppose that we must wait for a great deal of money before we can do anything. Perseverance is often better than a full purse. Many people fall behind, or miss the way altogether, because they do not perceive the simple and abundant means of getting on which surround them on every side;

The hand of the diligent maketh rich.

The integrity of the upright shall guide them.

Money is a good servant, but a bad master.

and it very often happens that these means are aids which can be had for the taking, but which money could not purchase.

Those who really wish to get on in the world, in every sense of the word, must have a large stock of patience and perseverance, of hopeful faith and confidence, be willing to learn and profit by the experiences which may be learned every day from nearly every person with whom they come in contact; and, above all, a disposition not easily cast down by difficulties and disappointments.

Rules for Reading.

READ the best books which wise and sensible persons advise, and study them with reflection and examination—that is, ask yourself, Do I understand what I read? Do I benefit by it? Do I become wiser and better thereby? Read with a firm determination to make use of all you read. Do not, by reading, neglect a more immediate or more important duty; do not read with a view of making a display of your reading. Do not read too much at a time. Reflect on what you have read, and let it be a nourishment of the heart and soul, moderately enjoyed and well digested.

Lavater.

Who begins amiss ends amiss.

WILD YOUNG MEN.

THERE is a class of young men who consider themselves gentlemen, and who are received by many as if they were; and yet they deserve as well to be sent to the treadmill or to the hulks as any scoundrel who receives sentence at the Old Bailey. These are they whom partial acquaintances, or persons of weak principle, or of none, call "wild young men." Now, their wildness is the least objectionable thing about them. They are almost vain and heartless to the last degree; and, however desperate in their extravagance, they are cool and calculating enough in their selfishness. These are the reckless villains who break the hearts of widowed mothers, and seem to feel no remorse for it. They have no notion of affection save as a weakness in a parent or a friend, of which they make advantage to obtain money for gross indulgences. These are the monsters who, even after they have come to years in which some honest thoughtfulness and some manly feeling might be expected, go on in a base career of blackguardism, which they are so wicked and so miserable as to think spirited, and dashing, and so forth. Meanwhile, mothers' hearts are breaking, and sisters are made ashamed, and fathers become morose and despairing of all good.

As you sow, so must you reap.

The mouth of the foolish is near destruction.

The sight of means to do ill-deeds makes ill-deeds done.

A prating fool shall fall.

and domestic circles, which might be full of thankfulness and cheerfulness and hope, are, by the hardened profligacy of one of their number, turned into gloom, and gnawing anxiety, and terrified anticipation of what each new day may bring forth.

And they who do this shocking mischief for their own gratification are merely called "wild young men!" What are they but robbers of the household store, ay, and too frequently parricides also, killing father and mother by inches, bringing down grey hairs with sorrow to the grave? The hangman's whip would be the most appropriate tamer of such wildness.

"THE TABLE-TALKER."

A GOOD NAME.

TWO of the most precious things on this side of the grave are life and reputation; and yet, strange to tell, the weakest weapon or an apparently trifling accident may deprive us of the first, and a contemptible whisper may be the means of our losing the second! Be more anxious therefore, young men, to deserve a good name rather than to possess one.

The memory of the just is blessed.

Do one thing at a time.

SIR FOWELL BUXTON.

YOU are now at that period of life in which you must make a turn to the right or to the left. You must now give proofs of principle, determination, and strength of mind—or you must sink into idleness, and acquire the habits and character of a desultory, ineffective young man; and, if once you fall to that point, you will find it no easy matter to rise again.

I am sure that a young man may be very much what he pleases. In my own case it was so. I left school, where I had learned little or nothing, about the age of fourteen. I spent the next year at home, learning to hunt and shoot. Then it was that the prospect of going to college opened upon me, and such thoughts as I have expressed in this letter occurred to my mind. I made my resolutions, and I acted up to them. I gave up all desultory reading—I never looked into a novel or newspaper—I gave up shooting. During the five years I was in Ireland, I had the liberty of going when I pleased to a capital shooting-place. I never went but twice. In short, I considered every hour as precious, and I made everything bend to my determination not to be behind any of my companions; and then I speedily passed from one species of character to another. I had been a boy

When you are a hammer, strike; when you are an anvil, bear.

Strive not with a man without cause.

Man proposes, God disposes.

Better late than never.

ond of pleasure and idleness, reading only books of unprofitable entertainment. I became speedily a youth of steady habits of application, and of irresistible resolution.

I soon gained the ground I had lost, and I found those things which were difficult, and almost impossible to my idleness, easy enough to my industry; and much of my happiness and all my *prosperity in life* have resulted from the change I made at your age.

If you seriously resolve to be energetic and industrious, depend upon it you will, for your whole life, have reason to rejoice that you were wise enough to form and to act upon that determination.

Sir Fowell Buxton's Motto.

THE longer I live, the more I am certain that the great difference between men—between the feeble and the powerful, the great and the insignificant—is ENERGY, INVINCIBLE DETERMINATION—a purpose once fixed, and then DEATH OR VICTORY. That quality will do anything that can be done in this world; and no talents, no circumstances, no opportunities, will make a two-legged creature a man without it.

Where no counsel is, the people fall.

GOODNESS OF HEART.

MY son, defraud not the poor of his living, and make not the needy eyes to wait long. Make not an hungry soul sorrowful; neither provoke a man in his distress.

Add not more trouble to an heart that is vexed; and defer not to give to him that is in need.

Reject not the supplication of the afflicted; neither turn away thy face from a poor man.

Turn not away thine eye from the needy, and give him none occasion to curse thee: for if he curse thee in the bitterness of his soul, his prayer shall be heard of him that made him.

Get thyself the love of the congregation, and bow thy head to a great man.

Let it not grieve thee to bow thine ear to the poor, and give him a friendly answer with meekness.

Deliver him that suffereth wrong from the hand of the oppressor; and be not faint-hearted when thou sittest in judgment.

Be as a father unto the fatherless, and instead of an husband unto their mother: so shalt thou be as the son of the Most High, and he shall love thee more than thy mother doeth.

Wisdom exalteth her children, and layeth hold of them that seek her.

Example is better than precept.

He that loveth her loveth life; and they that seek to her early shall be filled with joy.

He that holdeth her fast shall inherit glory; and wheresoever she entereth, the Lord will bless.

ECCLESIASTICUS.

THE POWER OF EXAMPLE.

PRESENT example gets within our guard,
    And acts with double force, by few repell'd.
    Ambition fires ambition; love of gain
    Strikes, like a pestilence, from breast to breast;
    Riot, pride, perfidy, blue vapours breathe;
And inhumanity is caught from man—
Smiling man. A slight, a single glance,
And shot at random, often has brought home
A sudden fever, to the throbbing heart,
Of envy, rancour, or impure desire.
We see, we hear with peril; safety dwells
Remote from multitude; the world's a school
Of wrong, and what proficients swarm around!
We must or imitate, or disapprove;
Must list as their accomplices, or foes;
That stains our innocence; this wounds our peace.
From nature's birth, hence, wisdom has been smit
With sweet recess, and languish'd for the shade.

EDWARD YOUNG.

The multitude of the wise is the welfare of the world.

The mouth of the just bringeth forth wisdom.

Believe not all you hear.

A friend in need is a friend indeed.

Companionship.

EVERY young man is the better for cherishing strong friendships with the wise and good; and he whose soul is knit to one or more chosen associates, with whom he can sympathise in right aims and feelings, is thereby the better armed against temptation and confirmed in paths of virtue.

But there is a trait that is far more exalted than the love of one's friends, and that is love to an enemy. The best of men are liable, by their very virtues, to provoke the hostility of the envious and malicious; and from the time of which it is significantly written, "Saul eyed David from that day forward," he was hunted by this degenerate king with a ruthless and a relentless hate; yet, after enduring an almost unparalleled series of persecutions from him, no sooner does he find Saul than he makes it an occasion for the display of a forbearance that is yet more unparalleled. Twice does he thus spare the life that is spent in hot pursuit of his own blood; and when Saul dies under other hands, he not only mourns him in touching elegy, but sternly avenges his death upon his murderer.

How different is this from that standard of worldly honour which calls resentment manly, and brands

A faithful friend is hard to find.

Be slow in choosing friends; slower in changing them.

Do good to them that hate you.

A little leaven, leavens a great mass.

with cowardice the lofty heart that, instead of meanly crushing its enemy, dares to conquer itself, and thereby achieves the greater victory over its foe!

He who cherishes this spirit of kindheartedness and magnanimity, governed by Christian principle, cannot fail to become a worthy, useful, and beloved member of society. He has in his possession the key that will unlock all hearts, though they be barred against him; and the means not only of his own temporal advancement, but what is better still, of discharging with fidelity his weighty responsibilities to others. COLLYER.

DOING GOOD.

HOW often do we sigh for opportunities of doing good, whilst we neglect the openings of Providence in little things, which would frequently lead to the accomplishment of most important usefulness! Dr. Johnson used to say "He who waits to do a great deal of good at once, will never do any." Good is done by degrees. However small in proportion the benefit which follows *individual attempts* to do good, a great deal may thus be accomplished by perseverance, even in the midst of discouragements and disappointments.

CRABBE.

A wise man is strong.

The glory of the law is justice.

Sir M. Hale's Resolutions.

THE character of Sir Matthew Hale as a judge was splendidly pre-eminent. His learning was profound; his patience unconquerable; his integrity stainless. In the words of one who wrote with no friendly feeling towards him, "his voice was oracular, and his person little less than adored." The temper of mind with which he entered upon the duties of the bench is best exemplified in the following resolutions, which appear to have been composed on his being raised to the dignity of Chief Baron, at the Restoration :—

"Things necessary to be continually had in remembrance :

"1. That in the administration of justice I am entrusted for God, the king, and country ; and therefore,

"2. That it be done, 1. Uprightly; 2. Deliberately; 3. Resolutely.

"3. That I rest not upon my own understanding or strength, but implore and rest upon the direction and strength of God.

"4. That in the execution of justice I carefully lay aside my own passions, and not give way to them, however provoked.

"5. That I be wholly intent upon the business

Law-makers should not be law-breakers.

The mouth of a righteous man is a well of life.

A man of understanding holdeth his peace.

Righteousness tendeth to life.

I am about, remitting all other cares and thoughts as unseasonable and interruptions.

"6. That I suffer not myself to be prepossessed with any judgment at all, till the whole business and both parties be heard.

"7. That I never engage myself in the beginning of any cause, but reserve myself unprejudiced till the whole be heard.

"8. That in business capital, though my nature prompt me to pity, yet to consider there is a pity also due to the country.

"9. That I be not too rigid in matters purely conscientious, where all the harm is diversity of judgment.

"10. That I be not biassed with compassion to the poor, or favour to the rich, in point of justice.

"11. That popular or court applause or distaste have no influence in anything I do, in point of distribution of justice.

"12. Not to be solicitous what men will say or think, so long as I keep myself exactly according to the rule of justice.

"13. If in criminals it be a measuring cast, to incline to mercy and acquittal.

"14. In criminals that consist merely in words, where no more harm ensues, moderation is no injustice.

"15. In criminals of blood, if the fact be evident, severity is justice.

The virtue of silence is a great piece of knowledge.

The Lord layeth up sound wisdom for the righteous.

The desire of the righteous is only good.

A righteous man hateth lying.

"16. To abhor all private solicitations, of what kind soever, and by whomsoever, in matters depending.

"17. To charge my servants, 1. Not to interpose in any matter whatsoever; 2. Not to take more than their known fees; 3. Not to give any undue precedence to causes; 4. Not to recommend counsel.

"18. To be short and sparing at meals, that I may be the fitter for business."

Make a Beginning.

REMEMBER in all things that if you do not begin you will never come to an end. The first weed pulled up in the garden, the first seed put in the ground, the first shilling put in the savings-bank, and the first mile travelled on a journey are all very important things. They make a beginning, and thereby a hope, a promise, a pledge, an assurance that you are in earnest with what you have undertaken.

How many a poor, idle, erring, hesitating outcast is now creeping and crawling his way through the world, who might have held up his head and prospered if, instead of putting off his resolutions of amendment and industry, he had only made a beginning!

A good beginning makes a good ending.

Hear the words of the wise.

THE CULTIVATION OF ENERGY.

THE cultivation of energy is of the greatest importance; resolute determination in the pursuit of worthy objects being the foundation of all true greatness of character. Energy enables a man to force his way through irksome drudgery and dry details, and carries him onward and upward in every station in life. It accomplishes more than genius, with not one-half the disappointment and peril. It is not eminent talent that is required to ensure success in any pursuit, so much as purpose; not merely the power to achieve, but the will to labour energetically and perseveringly. Hence energy of will may be defined to be the very central power of character in a man—in a word, it is the Man himself. It gives impulse to his every action, and soul to every effort. True hope is based on it; and it is hope that gives the real perfume to life. There is a fine heraldic motto on a broken helmet in Bolton Abbey, *L'espoir est ma force*, which might be the motto of every man's life. "Woe unto him that is faint-hearted," says the son of Sirach. There is, indeed, no blessing equal to the possession of a stout heart. Even if a man fail in his efforts, it will be a great satisfaction to him to enjoy the consciousness of having done his best. In humble life, nothing can be more cheering and beautiful

Force without foresight availeth little.

Energy is the motive power of character.

Labour is life.

than to see a man combating suffering by patience, triumphing in his integrity, and who, when his feet are bleeding and his limbs failing him, still walks upon his courage.

Mere wishes and desires but engender a sort of green-sickness in young minds, unless they are promptly embodied in act and deed. The good purpose once formed must be carried out with alacrity, and without swerving. In many walks of life, drudgery and toil must be cheerfully endured, as the necessary discipline of life. Hugh Miller says the only school in which he was properly taught, was "that world-wide school in which toil and hardship are the severe but noble teachers." He who allows his application to falter, or shirks his work on frivolous pretexts, is on the sure road to ultimate failure. Let any task be undertaken as a thing not possible to be evaded, and it will soon come to be performed with alacrity and cheerfulness. The habit of strenuous continued labour will become comparatively easy in time, like every other habit. Thus even men with the commonest brains and the most slender powers will accomplish much, if they will but apply themselves wholly and indefatigably to one thing at a time. Fowell Buxton placed his confidence in ordinary means and extraordinary application, realising the Scriptural injunction, "Whatsoever thy hand findeth to do, do it with all thy might;" and he himself

Whatsoever thy hand findeth to do,

attributed his own remarkable success in life to his practice of constantly "being a whole man to one thing at a time." SAMUEL SMILES.

COUNSEL TO WORKERS.

THERE is only one way that is safe for any man, or any number of men, by which they can maintain their present position if it be a good one, or raise themselves above it if it be a bad one—that is, by the practice of the virtues of industry, frugality, temperance, and honesty. There is no royal road by which men can raise themselves from a position which they feel to be uncomfortable and unsatisfactory, as regards their mental and physical condition, except by the practice of these virtues, by which they find numbers amongst them are continually advancing and bettering themselves. What is it that has made, that has in fact created, the "middle class" in this country, but the virtues to which I have alluded? There was a time when there was hardly any class in England, except the highest, that was equal to the poorest class at this moment.

How is it that the hundreds of thousands of

The heart of the prudent getteth knowledge.

There shall no evil happen to the just.

Do it with all thy might.

God helps them

Wealth gotten by vanity shall be diminished.

He that gathereth by labour shall increase.

men now existing in this our country, of the middle class, are educated, comfortable, and enjoying an amount of happiness and independence to which our forefathers were wholly unaccustomed? Why, by the practice of those very virtues; for I maintain that there has never been in any former age as much of these virtues as is now to be found amongst the great middle class of our community. When I speak of the middle class, I mean that class which is between the privileged class—the richest—and the very poorest in the community; and I would recommend every man to pay no attention whatever to public writers or speakers, whoever they may be, who tell them that this class or that class, that this law or that law, that this government or that government, can do all these things for them. I assure you, after long reflection and much observation, that there is no way for the working classes of this country to improve their condition but that which so many of them have already availed themselves of—that is, by the practice of those virtues, and by reliance upon themselves.

JOHN BRIGHT.

That help themselves.

Do not be above your business.

EARNESTNESS IN WORK.

IT ought to be a first principle, in beginning life, to do with earnestness what we have got to do. If it is worth doing at all, it is worth doing earnestly. If it is to be done well at all, it must be done with purpose and devotion.

Whatever may be our profession, let us mark all its bearings and details, its principles, its instruments, its applications. There is nothing about it should escape our study. There is nothing in it either too high or too low for our observation and knowledge. While we remain ignorant of any part of it, we are so far crippled in its use; we are liable to be taken at a disadvantage. This may be the very point the knowledge of which is most needed in some crisis, and those versed in it will take the lead, while we must be content to follow at a distance.

Our business, in short, must be the main drain of our intellectual activities day by day. It is the channel we have chosen for them; they must follow in it with a diffusive energy, filling every nook and corner. This is a fair test of professional earnestness. When we find our thoughts running after our business, and fixing themselves with a familiar fondness upon its details, we may be pretty sure of our way. When we find them

Industry is a good fire for cold limbs.

Employment brings enjoyment.

Idleness is the mother of vice.

running elsewhere, and only resorting with difficulty to the channel prepared for them, we may be equally sure we have taken a wrong turn. We cannot be earnest about anything which does not naturally and strongly engage our thoughts.

PRINCIPAL TULLOCH.

IMPORTANCE OF LITTLE THINGS.

THE dictionary definition of Business shows how large a part of practical life arranges itself under this head. It is, "Employment; an affair; serious engagement; something to be transacted; something required to be done." Every human being has duties to be performed; and, therefore, has need of cultivating the capacity for doing them; whether the sphere of action be the management of a household, the conduct of a trade or profession, or the government of a nation.

Attention, application, accuracy, method, punctuality, and dispatch are the principal qualities required for efficiently conducting business of any sort. These, at first sight, may appear to be small matters; and yet they are of essential importance to human

The wise man's eyes are in his head:

happiness, well-being, and usefulness. They are little things, it is true; but human life is made up of comparative trifles. It is the repetition of little acts which constitutes not only the sum of human character, but which determines the character of nations; and where men or nations have broken down, it will almost invariably be found that neglect of little things was the rock on which they split.

It is related of a well-known Manchester manufacturer that, on retiring from business, he purchased a large estate from a noble lord; and it was part of the arrangement that he was to take the house, with all its furniture, precisely as it stood. On taking possession, however, he found that a cabinet, which was in the inventory, had been removed; and on applying to the former owner about it, the latter said, "Well, I certainly did order it to be removed; but I hardly thought you would have cared for so trifling a matter in so large a purchase." "My lord," was the characteristic reply, "if I had not all my life attended to trifles, I should not have been able to purchase this estate; and—excuse me for saying so—perhaps if your lordship had cared more about trifles, you might not have had occasion to sell it."

SAMUEL SMILES.

But the fool walketh in darkness.

Be not among wine-bibbers;

Franklin's Virtues.

1. TEMPERANCE.—Eat not to dullness; drink not to elevation.

2. SILENCE.—Speak not but what may benefit others or yourself; avoid trifling conversation.

3. ORDER.—Let all things have their places; let each part of your business have its time.

4. RESOLUTION.—Resolve to perform what you ought; perform without fail what you resolve.

5. FRUGALITY.—Make no expense but to do good to others or yourself; that is, waste nothing.

6. INDUSTRY.—Lose no time; be always employed in something useful; cut off all unnecessary actions.

7. SINCERITY.—Use no hurtful deceit; think innocently and justly; and if you speak, speak accordingly.

8. JUSTICE.—Wrong none by doing injuries, or omitting the benefits that are your duty.

9. MODERATION.—Avoid extremes; forbear resenting injuries as much as you think they deserve.

10. CLEANLINESS.—Tolerate no uncleanliness in body, clothes, or habitation.

11. TRANQUILLITY.—Be not disturbed at trifles, or at accidents, common or unavoidable.

12. CHASTITY.   13. HUMILITY.

Where no counsel is, the people fall

The lip of truth shall be established for ever.

Among riotous eaters of the flesh.

POINTS OF MANLINESS.

TRUE manliness is power to say to the solicitations of evil, come in what form they may, "Get thee behind me, Satan." George Washington showed himself a man at the age of thirteen. Among the rules he then adopted for his conduct through life, we find these: "Learn to keep alive in your breast that little spark of celestial fire called conscience." "Let your recreations be manful, not sinful." And to show his regard for a sincere piety, he wrote thus: "When you speak of God, or His attributes, let it be done seriously, and with reverence."

Next to devotion to God, true manliness demands fidelity to our race. To maltreat any human being is to insult the image of God. The more truly we honour all men—the labourer no less than the capitalist, the humble equally with the most exalted—the more ready we are to act well our part as neighbours, citizens, patriots, and philanthropists—the greater is our manliness.

The youthful period of life is interesting for the strength of will it usually exhibits. That strength may, it is true, be given to the service of sin. It is melancholy to observe how juvenile offenders have increased in our courts of justice; the annals of crime in our time, and in many cities, are crowded with youthful names.

We never contemplate the mighty forces of youth without joining in the sentiment, " Precious is youthful energy, may it be preserved till the temple of virtue and truth is reached!" But, alas! all along he must advance through an avenue of tempters and demons, all prompt to touch him, and draw away that divine, electric element with which he is charged.

Another characteristic of young men is independence. They think for themselves, in the main, more than childhood can, more than manhood generally does. They may, and often do, make mistakes; but we sometimes feel that it is better to fall into a little error occasionally, when thinking for one's self, than to keep mechanically and imitatively right. "As a living dog is better than a dead lion," so he who has a root in himself is likely to recover from his errors and follies.

An independent man is a real man, and real men are what is required in this world. It is easy for a man to lose his soul in the forms around him. To know any of these as realities, we must begin by being real in our own will, conscience, and personal energy. Then we may go on through eternity, gradually deeper and deeper, into endless diversities of direction, and into a region of inexhaustible realities.

Truth is the best speech.

DUTY UNIVERSAL.

DUTY is a thing that is due, and must be paid by every man who would avoid present discredit and eventual moral insolvency. It is an obligation—a debt—which can only be discharged by voluntary effort and resolute action in the affairs of life.

Duty embraces man's whole existence. It begins in the home, where there is the duty which children owe to their parents on the one hand, and the duty which parents owe to their children on the other. There are, in like manner, the respective duties of husbands and wives, of masters and servants; while outside the home there are the duties which men and women owe to each other as friends and neighbours, as employers and employed, as governors and governed.

"Render, therefore," says St. Paul, "to all their dues: tribute to whom tribute is due; custom to whom custom; fear to whom fear; honour to whom honour. Owe no man anything, but to love one another; for he that loveth another hath fulfilled the law."

Thus duty rounds the whole of life, from our entrance into it until our exit from it — duty to

The hope of unjust men perisheth.

The rod and reproof give wisdom.

Let "duty" be thy watchword.

The three main duties of a Christian's life

superiors, duty to inferiors, and duty to equals — duty to man, and duty to God. Wherever there is power to use or to direct, there is duty. For we are but as stewards, appointed to employ the means entrusted to us for our own and for others' good.

The abiding sense of duty is the very crown of character. It is the upholding law of man in his highest attitudes. Without it, the individual totters and falls before the first puff of adversity or temptation; whereas, inspired by it, the weakest becomes strong and full of courage. "Duty," says Mrs. Jameson, "is the cement which binds the whole moral edifice together; without which, all power, goodness, intellect, truth, happiness, love itself, can have no permanence; but all the fabric of existence crumbles away from under us, and leaves us at last sitting in the midst of a ruin, astonished at our own desolation."

Duty is based upon a sense of justice — justice inspired by love, which is the most perfect form of goodness. Duty is not a sentiment, but a principle pervading the life: and it exhibits itself in conduct and in acts, which are mainly determined by man's conscience and freewill.

SAMUEL SMILES.

Abhor that which is evil.

Cleave to that which is good.

Are retrospection, inspection, and anticipation.

No sense like common sense.

THE WAY TO WEALTH.

AS an epitome of worldly wisdom, we know of no better than "The Way to Wealth, as clearly shown in the Preface of an old Pennsylvanian Almanac, entitled 'Poor Richard Improved,'" written by the great American philosopher, Benjamin Franklin. It is homely, simple, sensible, and practical—a condensation of the proverbial wit, wisdom, and every-day philosophy, useful at all times, and essentially so in the present day. Nearly every line contains a Good Device or a Precept for Practice, and we earnestly commend its perusal to our readers.

"COURTEOUS READER,—I have heard that nothing gives an author so great pleasure as to find his works respectfully quoted by others. Judge, then, how much I must have been gratified by an incident I am going to relate to you. I stopped my horse lately where a great number of people were collected at an auction of merchant's goods. The hour of the sale not being come, they were conversing on the badness of the times, and one of the company called to a plain, clean old man with white locks, 'Pray, Father Abraham, what think you of the times? Will not these heavy taxes quite ruin the country? How shall we ever be able to pay them? What would you advise us to do?' Father Abraham stood up, and replied, 'If you would have my advice I will give it you in short,

The used key is always bright.

He that lives upon hope may die fasting.

Spur metal is the best metal.

Hearken to good advice.

for, A word to the wise is enough, as poor Richard says.' They joined in desiring him to speak his mind, and gathering round him, he proceeded as follows :—

" 'Friends, the taxes are indeed very heavy, and if those laid on by the government were the only ones we had to pay we might more easily discharge them; but we have many others, and much more grievous to some of us. We are taxed twice as much by our idleness, three times as much by our pride, and four times as much by our folly; and from these taxes the commissioners cannot ease or deliver us, by allowing an abatement. However, let us hearken to good advice, and something may be done for us. God helps them that help themselves, as poor Richard says.

" 'I. It would be thought a hard government that should tax its people one-tenth part of their time, to be employed in its service; but idleness taxes many of us more; sloth, by bringing on diseases, absolutely shortens life. Sloth, like rust, consumes faster than labour wears; while, The used key is always bright, as poor Richard says. But, Dost thou love life, then do not squander time, for that is the stuff life is made of, as poor Richard says. How much more than is necessary do we spend in sleep! forgetting that, The sleeping fox catches no poultry; and that, There will be sleeping in the grave, as poor Richard says.

" 'If time be of all things the most precious, wasting time must be, as poor Richard says, the greatest prodigality; since, as he elsewhere tells us, Lost time is never found again; and, What we call time enough always proves little enough. Let us, then, be up and be doing, and doing to the purpose; so by diligence shall we do more, and with less perplexity. Sloth makes all things difficult, but industry

Time lost is never found again.

The present time is our own.

A word to the wise is enough.

all easy; and, He that riseth late must trot all day, and shall scarce overtake his business at night; while, Laziness travels so slowly that poverty soon overtakes him. Drive thy business, let not that drive thee; and, Early to bed, and early to rise, makes a man healthy, wealthy, and wise, as poor Richard says.

" 'So what signifies wishing and hoping for better times? We may make these times better if we bestir ourselves. Industry need not risk, and, He that lives upon hopes will die fasting. There are no gains without pains; then, Help, hands, for I have no lands; or, if I have, they are smartly taxed. He that hath a trade, hath an estate; and, He that hath a calling, hath an office of profit and honour, as poor Richard says; but then the trade must be worked at, and the calling followed, or neither the estate nor the office will enable us to pay our taxes. If we are industrious we shall never starve; for, At the working man's house, hunger looks in, but dares not enter. Nor will the bailiff or the constable enter; for, Industry pays debts, while despair increaseth them. What though you have found no treasure, nor has any rich relation left you a legacy? Diligence is the mother of good luck, and God gives all things to industry. Then, Plough deep, while sluggards sleep, and you shall have corn to sell and to keep. Work while it is called to-day, for you know not how much you may be hindered to-morrow. One to-day is worth two to-morrows, as poor Richard says; and, further, Never leave that till to-morrow what you can do to-day. If you were a servant, would you not be ashamed that a good master should catch you idle? Are you then your own master, be ashamed to catch yourself idle, when there is to be so much done for yourself, your family, your country, and your king. Handle your tools without mittens;

remember that the cat in gloves catches no mice, as poor Richard says. It is true there is much to be done, and perhaps you are weak-handed; but stick to it steadily, and you will see great effects; for, Constant dropping wears away stones; and, By diligence and patience the mouse ate in two the cable; and, Little strokes fell great oaks.

"'Methinks I hear some of you say, "Must a man afford himself no leisure?" I will tell thee, my friend, what poor Richard says—Employ thy time well if thou meanest to gain leisure; and since thou art not sure of a minute, throw not away an hour. Leisure is time for doing something useful. This leisure the diligent man will obtain, but the lazy man never; for a life of leisure and a life of laziness are two things. Many, without labour, would live by their wits only, but they break for want of stock; whereas industry gives comfort, and plenty, and respect. Fly pleasures, and they will follow you. The diligent spinner has a large shift; and, Now I have a sheep and a cow, everybody bids me good-morrow.

"'II. But with our industry we must likewise be steady, settled, and careful, and oversee our own affairs with our own eyes, and not trust too much to others; for, as poor Richard says—

"'I never saw an oft-removèd tree,
Nor yet an oft-removèd family,
That throve so well as those that settled be.

And again—Three removes are as bad as a fire. And again—Keep thy shop, and thy shop will keep thee. And again—If you would have your business done, go; if not, send. And again—

"'He that by the plough would thrive,
Himself must either hold or drive.

A man's own care is profitable.

And again—The eye of a master will do more work than both his hands. And again—Want of care does us more damage than want of knowledge. And again—Not to oversee workmen is to leave them your purse open. Trusting too much to others' care is the ruin of many; for, in the affairs of this world, men are saved, not by faith, but by the want of it. But a man's own care is profitable; for if you would have a faithful servant, and one that you like, serve yourself. A little neglect may cause great mischief; For want of a nail the shoe was lost; for want of a shoe the horse was lost; for want of a horse the rider was lost, being overtaken and slain by the enemy—all for want of a little care about a horse-shoe nail.

" 'III. So much for industry, my friends, and attention to one's own business; but to these we must add frugality, if we would make our industry more certainly successful. A man may, if he knows not how to save as he gets, keep his nose to the grindstone all his life, and die not worth a groat at last. A fat kitchen makes a lean will; and

" ' Many estates are spent in the getting,
   Since women for tea forsook spinning and knitting,
   And men for punch forsook hewing and splitting.

If you would be wealthy, think of saving as well as of getting. The Indies have not made Spain rich, because her outgoes are greater than her incomes.

" 'Away, then, with your expensive follies, and you will not then have so much cause to complain of hard times, heavy taxes, and chargeable families; for

" 'Women and wine, game and deceit,
   Make the wealth small and the want great.

And further—What maintains one vice would bring up two

No gains without pains.

Plough deep while sluggards sleep,

children. You may think, perhaps, that a little tea, or a little punch, now and then, diet a little more costly, clothes a little finer, and a little entertainment now and then, can be no great matter; but remember—Many a little makes a mickle. Beware of little expenses—A small leak will sink a great ship, as poor Richard says. And again—Who dainties love shall beggars prove. And moreover—Fools make feasts, and wise men eat them.

"'Here you are all got together at this sale of fineries and nick-nacks. You call them goods; but if you do not take care they will prove evils to some of you. You expect they will be sold cheap, and perhaps they may for less than they cost; but if you have no occasion for them they must be dear to you. Remember what poor Richard says—Buy what thou hast no need of, and ere long thou shalt sell thy necessaries. And again—At a great pennyworth pause awhile. He means that the cheapness is apparent only, and not real; or the bargain, by straitening thee in thy business, may do thee more harm than good; for in another place he says—Many have been ruined by buying good pennyworths. Again—It is foolish to lay out money in a purchase of repentance; and yet this folly is practised every day at auctions, for want of minding the almanack. Many a one, for the sake of finery on the back, has gone with a hungry belly and half-starved his family. Silks and satins, scarlet and velvets, put out the kitchen fire, as poor Richard says. These are not the necessaries of life; they can scarcely be called the conveniences; and yet, only because they look pretty, how many want to have them! By these, and other extravagances, the genteel are reduced to poverty, and forced to borrow of those whom they formerly despised, but who, through industry and frugality, have maintained their stand-

Who dainties love shall beggars prove.

Nothing is cheap that you do not want.

And you shall have corn to sell and keep.

Never leave that till to-morrow

ing; in which case it appears plainly that, A ploughman on his legs is higher than a gentleman on his knees, as poor Richard says. Perhaps they have had a small estate left them, which they knew not the getting of; they think it is day, and will never be night; that a little to be spent out of so much is not worth minding; but, Always taking out of the meal-tub, and never putting in, soon comes to be the bottom, as poor Richard says; and then, When the well is dry, they know the worth of water. But this they might have known before if they had taken his advice—If you would know the value of money, go and try to borrow some; for, He that goes a-borrowing goes a-sorrowing, as poor Richard says; and, indeed, so does he that lends to such people when he goes to get his own in again. Poor Dick further advises, and says—

> "'Fond pride of dress is sure a very curse;
> Ere fancy you consult, consult your purse.

And again—Pride is as loud a beggar as want, and a great deal more saucy. When you have bought one fine thing, you must buy ten more, that your appearance may be all of a piece; but poor Dick says, It is easier to suppress the first desire, than to satisfy all that follow it. And it is as truly folly for the poor to ape the rich, as for the frog to swell in order to equal the ox.

> "'Vessels large may venture more,
> But little boats should keep near shore.

It is, however, a folly soon punished; for, as poor Richard says, Pride that dines on vanity, sups on contempt. Pride breakfasted with plenty, dined with poverty, and supped with infamy. And, after all, of what use is this pride of appearance, for which so much is risked, so much is

Want of care does more damage than want of knowledge.

Pride is as loud a beggar as want.

What you can do to-day.

> He that by the plough would thrive,

suffered? It cannot promote health, nor ease pain; it makes no increase of merit in the person; it creates envy; it hastens misfortune.

"'But what madness must it be to run in debt for these superfluities! We are offered, by the terms of this sale, six months' credit; and that, perhaps, has induced some of us to attend it, because we cannot spare the ready money, and hope now to be fine without it. But, ah! think what you do when you run in debt; you give to another power over your liberty. If you cannot pay at the time, you will be ashamed to see your creditor; you will be in fear when you speak to him; you will make poor, pitiful, sneaking excuses, and, by degrees, come to lose your veracity, and sink into base, downright lying; for, The second vice is lying, the first is running in debt, as poor Richard says; and again, to the same purpose, Lying rides upon debt's back. . . . .

"'And now, to conclude—Experience keeps a dear school, but fools will learn in no other, as poor Richard says, and scarce in that; for, it is true, We may give advice, but we cannot give conduct. However, remember this—They that will not be counselled, cannot be helped; and further, that, If you will not hear Reason, she will surely rap your knuckles, as poor Richard says.'

"Thus the old gentleman ended his harangue. The people heard it and approved the doctrine; and immediately practised the contrary, just as if it had been a common sermon, for the auctioneer opened, and they began to buy extravagantly. I found the good man had thoroughly studied my almanacks, and digested all I had dropt on these topics during the course of twenty-five years. The frequent mention he made of me must have tired any one

(margin left: Lying rides upon debt's back.)
(margin right: Despair increaseth debt.)

> Himself must either hold or drive.

else; but my vanity was wonderfully delighted with it, though I was conscious that not a tenth part of the wisdom was my own which he had ascribed to me, but rather the gleanings that I had made of the sense of all ages and nations. However, I resolved to be the better for the echo of it; and though I had at first determined to buy stuff for a new coat, I went away resolved to wear my old one a little longer. Reader, if thou wilt do the same, thy profit will be as great as mine. "RICHARD SAUNDERS."

THE MANLINESS OF RELIGION.

RELIGION is the manliest of all things. There may be those who associate it with what is feeble and effeminate; who deem it a man's highest honour to be intellectual, clever, accomplished, learned; but who look with a half-contemptuous tolerance on pious feeling, as a thing for women and children. Religion is indeed a thing for the gentlest and the lowliest, in which the simplest and sweetest natures find all that is congenial to them; but it is not the less that which may claim kindred with the loftiest culture, to which the richest treasures of thought and learning may well be offered up. Its language is that which babes may lisp, but it is also that which the lips of sages may not disdain to utter. Felt in the heart of childhood, it is the last and highest secret of a man's strength and power.

It is manly to be devout. For it is religion which elicits that which is highest and grandest in man's nature; touches and wakes to life springs of thought and feeling which had lain dormant else; elevates, transfigures, harmonises all the elements of our being, and whatever we may have been before, makes us double the men we were.

It is manly to be religious. For it is religion which widens thought; gives to us the most far-reaching views of the world and human life; and raises the soul in which it dwells above the shifting sands of time, above the weary dust and din and clatter of life's passing interests, above its mean aims and sordid motives and petty ambitions, far, far above and beyond its dreams and shadows, into communion and converse with the Eternal Reality.

It is manly to be religious. For it is our religion, our Christian faith which brings us into fellowship with Him who is the One Man of all time, the perfect ideal of humanity, the Being in whom the hidden possibilities of manhood were disclosed, before the splendour of whose moral loveliness all that has ever been of human nobleness and heroism seems commonplace, whose character shames our weaknesses and fills us with wholesome detestation of our sins, and to follow whom—faintly, distantly, fitfully, with far-off and uncertain steps though it be—is the one worthiest aim of human existence.

Trust in the Lord at all times.

Say then, if all this be so—if it be true, as I boldly affirm it is, that to be religious is to be thoughtful and brave and pure and free, to have the clear calm mind, the soul upright and true, the generous, tender, tolerant heart, the resolute will which no temptation of interest or passion can bribe or shake; if it be religious to discern the deep meaning of man's life, to enter with earnestness and with zest into its everyday duties; yet when with advancing years the ever-lengthening shadow begins to fall deeper and darker on our path, or when the sharp call of sudden sickness summons us to meet our doom, to be able to face it calmly, quietly, undismayed, with a man's courageous heart; oh, if this be so, may I not, with a deep, solemn significance, say, "Brethren, be no longer children in understanding: howbeit, in malice be ye children, but in understanding be men!"

PROFESSOR CAIRD.

Inexperience.

INEXPERIENCE is a rock on which many a youth strikes, and makes shipwreck of his prospects of advancement in life. It has been said that we learn nothing truly valuable except from experience. If so, what perils must lie on the threshold of life! A single wrong step, as we cross it, may cause us to stumble

He that keepeth the law, happy is he.

The counsel of the Lord standeth for ever.

Depart from evil and do good.

The tongue deviseth mischiefs.

and fall; it may be never to rise again, hopelessly excluded from the high niche we might otherwise have filled in the temple, not only of honour and profit, but what is of far more value and importance, of personal purity and dignity of character. In the morning of life, imagination and passion run their wildest and their widest races; while reason and experience, developed as years pass over our heads, and making us all-controlling and all-decisive, are as yet immature. That self-poised vigour, which age alone can impart, is as yet wanting. Man is, to a great extent, a creature of imitation; easily he catches the tone of thought and conduct of those he comes in contact with. How careful, therefore, ought every youth be to observe that he learns experience from the really good and wise men of the world, and shun the lessons to be gained from the experience of those who are low and unprincipled in conduct and morality!

Let us not be weary in well-doing.

One sinner destroyeth much good.

THERE is a tide in the affairs of men,
Which, taken at its flood, leads on to fortune;
Omitted, all the voyage of their life
Is bound in shallows, and in miseries.
On such a full sea are we now afloat:
And we must take the current as it serves,
Or lose our venture.   SHAKESPEARE.

Be not wise in thine own eyes.

Great men are not always wise.

THE BEST TEMPERAMENT.

ONE of the great aids or hindrances to success in anything lies in the temperament of a man. I do not know yours; but I venture to point out to you what is the best temperament, namely, a combination of the desponding and the resolute; or, as I had better express it, of the apprehensive and the resolute. Such is the temperament of great commanders. Secretly, they rely upon nothing and upon nobody. There is such a powerful element of failure in all human affairs, that a shrewd man is always saying to himself, "What shall I do if that which I count upon does not come out as I expect?" This foresight dwarfs and crushes all but men of great resolution.

Then be not over-choice in looking out for what may exactly suit you, but rather be ready to adopt any opportunities that occur. Fortune does not stoop often to take any one up. Favourable opportunities will not happen precisely in the way that you have imagined. Nothing does. Be not discouraged, therefore, by a present detriment in any course which may lead to something good. Time is so precious here.

Get, if you can, into one or other of the main grooves of human affairs. It is all the difference of

Strike while the iron is hot.

A man's pride shall bring him low.

Light without heat does little good.

going by railway and walking over a ploughed field, whether you adopt common sources or set up one for yourself. You will see, if your times are anything like ours, most inferior persons highly placed in the army, in the church, in office, at the bar. They have somehow got upon the line, and have moved on well, with very little original motive-power of their own. Do not let this make you talk as if merit were utterly neglected in these or any professions: only that getting well into the groove will frequently do instead of any great excellence.

* * * * * *

Whatever happens, do not be dissatisfied with your worldly fortunes, lest that speech be justly made to you, which was once made to a repining person much given to talk of how great she and hers had been— "Yes, madam," was the crushing reply, "we all find our level at last."

Eternally that fable is true, of a choice being given to men on their entrance into life. Two majestic women stand before you: one in rich vesture, superb with what seems a mural crown on her head, and plenty in her hand, and something of triumph, I will not say of boldness, in her eye; and she, the queen of this world, can give you many things. The other is beautiful, but not alluring, nor rich, nor powerful; and there are traces of care, and shame, and sorrow

Do that which is good,

in her face; and—marvellous to say—her look is downcast and yet noble. She can *give* you nothing, but she can *make* you somebody. If you cannot bear to part from her sweet, sublime countenance, which hardly veils with sorrow its infinity, follow her—follow her, I say, if you are really minded so to do; but do not, while you are on this track, look back with ill-concealed envy on the glittering things which fall in the path of those who prefer to follow the rich dame, and to pick up the riches and honours which fall from her cornucopia. This is, in substance, what a true artist said to me only the other day, impatient, as he told me, of the complaints of those who would pursue art, and yet have a fortune.

SIR ARTHUR HELPS.

BE merry, but with modesty; be sober, but not sullen; be valiant, but not venturous; let your clothes be comely, but not costly; your diet wholesome, but not excessive; mistrust no man without cause, neither be thou credulous without proof. Serve God, fear God, love God, and God will so bless you as either your heart can wish or your friends desire.

LYLY.

The hand of the diligent shall bear rule.

He that refuseth reproof erreth.

And thou shalt have praise.

Sir John Pakington's Three Rules.

I AM indebted for whatever measure of success I have attained in my public life, to a combination of moderate abilities with honesty of intention, firmness of purpose, and steadiness of conduct. If I were to offer advice to any young man anxious to make himself useful in public life, I would sum up the results of my experience in three short rules—rules so simple that any man may understand them, and so easy that any man may act upon them. My first rule will be, leave it to others to judge of what duties you are capable, and for what position you are fitted; but never refuse to give your services in whatever capacity it may be the opinion of others who are competent to judge that you may benefit your neighbours and your country. My second rule is, when you agree to undertake public duties, concentrate every energy and faculty in your possession with the determination to discharge those duties to the best of your ability. Lastly, I would counsel you that, in deciding on the line which you will take in public affairs, you should be guided in your decision by that which, after mature deliberation, you believe to be right, and not by that which, in the passing hour, may happen to be fashionable or popular.

RELIGION.

FOR thy religion, distinguish not thyself by be not factious for, nor serve under any sect whatever; be thou a Christian, the most pure, certain, noblest worshipper of God of all others. But if thou art pressed to give thy name up to any one profession, inquire after and embrace that whose principles conduce most to piety, that which comes nearest to the doctrine of Christ. And in the examination of questions in religion, though I am no divine, yet I dare venture to guide your conscience thus far. Be careful still to search into the consequences of a doctrine; rely upon the Scriptures which are, without exposition, plain; and which, if they offer injury to the attributes of God, rendering them such as we should abhor ourselves to be, or if they open the gate to looseness and profanity, by no means give them entertainment. Lastly, labour diligently to find the truth when God shall enable you with abilities for that great work, for I would not have you owe your religion to your education only; and for your encouragement to the search of this truth, heedfully remember the most excellent saying of our blessed Saviour—"If any man will do his will, he shall know of the doctrine whether it be of God or man."

A Sabbath well spent,

God never denied Himself to him that sought Him by prayer and holiness of life. And when you have thus happily found this divine truth, embrace it sincerely, and follow it constantly, and be sure to give it honour by your conversation.

EARL OF BEDFORD.

MAN AND CIRCUMSTANCES.

INSTEAD of saying that man is the creature of circumstance, it would be nearer the mark to say that man is the architect of circumstance. It is character which builds an existence out of circumstance. Our strength is measured by our plastic power. From the same materials one man builds palaces, another hovels; one warehouses, another villas. Bricks and mortar are mortar and bricks, until the architect can make them something else. Thus it is that in the same family, in the same circumstances, one man rears a stately edifice, while his brother, vacillating and incompetent, lives for ever amid ruins. The block of granite, which was an obstacle on the pathway of the weak, becomes a stepping-stone on the pathway of the strong.

G. H. LEWES.

Brings a week of content.

Evildoers shall be cut off.

The way of man is not in himself.

Bad Examples.

THERE are several kinds of bad examples that do us harm—namely, those we imitate, those we proudly exult over, those which drive us into an opposite extreme, and those which lower our standard. This last is the most hurtful. For one who is corrupted by becoming readily as bad as a very bad example, there are ten that are debased by being content with the idea that they are better than the worst. Nothing is so dangerous as to be perpetually measuring ourselves by what is beneath us; and being satisfied at feeling a superiority to that which, despite ourselves, we more and more assimilate. A great principle is involved in this statement. In judging things outward and secular, we act always in view of some particular standard. When we speak of an article as good or bad, there is a scale in our minds by which we measure it; and hence, what is sufficient in one estimate is insufficient in another. This principle applies equally to moral and spiritual things. To say of a man that he is a good man, implies that we judge him by some determinate standard. By another standard he may not be a good man; he may even be a bad man.

Trust not swearers,

Nothing, then, it will be perceived, is of more vital importance to those in youth and early manhood, than to adopt a true standard of moral and spiritual excellence. If you fail on this point, you may come to be satisfied with the very smallest moral attainments. Only bring your standard down low enough, and there is no point of degradation to which you may not sink, and still acquit yourself of guilt. Hence, the main safe-guard of character consists in keeping the rule by which we estimate ourselves at the greatest possible height; and in view of this vital truth, the Scriptures have given us a clear and definite standard—it is this: he only is truly good who is so when judged by the law of God.

*A*VOID *I*DLENESS.

AVOID idleness, and fill up all the spaces of thy time with severe and useful employment; for lust easily creeps in at those emptinesses where the soul is unemployed, and the body is at ease; for no easy, healthful, idle person was ever chaste if he could be tempted; but of all employments bodily labour is the most useful, and of the greatest benefit for driving away the devil. JEREMY TAYLOR.

Neither believe boasters.

Bad customs are not binding.

Better suffer wrong than do it.

Look to others, but trust to yourself.

SELF-RELIANCE.

INSIST on yourself; never imitate. Your own gift you can present every moment with the cumulative force of a whole life's cultivation; but of the adopted talent of another you have only an extemporaneous half-possession. That which each can do best, none but his Maker can teach him. No man yet knows what it is, nor can, till that person has exhibited it. Where is the master who could have taught Shakespeare? Where is the man who could have instructed Franklin, or Washington, or Bacon, or Newton? Every great man is a unique. The Scipionism of Scipio is precisely that part he could not borrow. If anybody will tell me whom the great man imitates in the original crisis when he performs a great act, I will tell him who else than himself can teach him. Shakespeare will never be made by the study of Shakespeare. Do that which is assigned thee, and thou canst not hope too much, or dare too much. There is at this moment for me an utterance bare and grand as that of the colossal chisel of Phidias, or trowel of the Egyptians, or the pen of Moses and Dante, but different from all these. Not possible will the soul, all rich, all eloquent with thousand-cloven tongue, deign to repeat itself; but if I can

"Can do" is easily carried about.

Eagles fly alone, but sheep herd together.

No help like self-help.

hear what these patriarchs say, surely I can reply in the same pitch of voice; for the ear and the tongue are two organs of one nature. Dwell up there in the simple and noble regions of thy life, obey the heart, and thou shalt reproduce the fore-world again.

EMERSON.

THE VALUE OF TRAVEL.

IT draws the grossness of the understanding,
And renders active and industrious spirits.
He that knows most men's manners must of necessity
Best know his own, and mend those by example.
'Tis a dull thing to travel like a mill-horse,
Still in the place he was born in, lamed, and blinded;
Living at home is like it. Pure and strong spirits,
That, like the fire, still covet to fly upward,
And to give fire as well as take it, cased up and mew'd here—
I mean at home, like lusty-mettled horses,
Only tied up in stables to please their masters,
Beat out their fiery lives in their own litters.

BEAUMONT AND FLETCHER.

EVIL ASSOCIATIONS.

OF all the dangers to which the young can be exposed, there is not one which experience pronounces more imminent than the company and example of the ungodly. "Sinners" are fond to have associates in their evil courses. Some of these courses are such as cannot be pursued without associates. And in how many instances besides is solitary vice—vice, of which the perpetrator has no companion but his own conscience, felt to be irksome and miserable! How often is it for the purpose of preventing the intrusions, and silencing the annoying whispers or louder remonstrances of this troublesome visitor, that company is courted! "Hand joins in hand." They keep one another in countenance; they rally each other's spirits; they drown dull care; they unite in "making a mock at sin." They help each other to "break God's bands asunder, and cast away his cords from them;" and, for the time at least, to give their foreboding fears to the winds. And while the fearers of God, in the exercise of a pure benevolence, rejoice with the angels of heaven over a repenting sinner—over one who turns from the "fatal paths of folly, sin, and death," into the paths of wisdom, purity, and peace—these children of the Wicked One

Blessed is the man that walketh not — In the counsel of the ungodly, — Nor standeth in the way of sinners, — Nor sitteth in the seat of the scornful.

participate in his infernal pleasure, when they succeed in seducing any from the right way, and thus obtaining an accession to their numbers, and an encouragement to their selfish indulgences, from the ranks of religion and virtue.

DR. WARDLAW.

THE EVIL OF POVERTY.

DO not accustom yourself to consider debt only as an inconvenience; you will find it a calamity. Poverty takes away so many means of doing good, and produces so much inability to resist evil, both natural and moral, that it is by all virtuous means to be avoided. Let it be your first care, then, not to be in any man's debt. Resolve not to be poor; whatever you have, spend less. Poverty is a great enemy to human happiness; it certainly destroys liberty, and it makes some virtues impracticable, and others extremely difficult. Frugality is not only the basis of quiet, but of beneficence. No man can help others that wants help himself; we must have enough before we have to spare.

DR. JOHNSON.

Honour and wealth from no condition rise;

DISHONOUR.

A MAN of business should be an honourable man. Although a man cannot be honourable without being honest, yet he may be strictly honest without being honourable. Honesty refers chiefly to pecuniary matters; honour applies to the principles and feelings. You may pay your debts punctually, you may defraud no man, and yet you may act dishonourably. You act dishonourably when you give your correspondents a worse opinion of your rivals in trade than you know they deserve. You act dishonourably when you sell your commodities at less than their real value, in order to attract your neighbour's customers. You act dishonourably when you purchase goods at higher than the market value, in order that you may raise the market upon another buyer. You act dishonourably when you negotiate accommodation bills with your bankers, as if they arose out of real transactions. You act dishonourably in every case wherein your outward conduct is at variance with your real opinions. You act dishonourably if, when carrying on a prosperous trade, you do not allow your servants and assistants, through whose exertions you obtain your success, to participate in your prosperity. You act

A safe conscience makes a sound sleep.

The wicked shall fall by his own wickedness.

Act well your part, there all the honour lies.

dishonourably if, after you have become rich, you are forgetful of the favours you received when poor. In all these cases there may be no intentional fraud; it may not be dishonest, but it is nevertheless dishonourable.

J. W. GILBART.

PROMPTITUDE IN BUSINESS.

BEWARE of stumbling over a propensity which easily besets you from not having your time fully employed—I mean what the women call *dawdling*. Your motto must be *Hoc age*. Do instantly whatever is to be done, and take the hours of recreation after business, never before it. When a regiment is under march, the rear is often thrown into confusion because the front do not move steadily and without interruption. It is the same with business; if that which is in hand is not instantly, steadily, and regularly dispatched, other things accumulate behind, till affairs begin to press all at once, and no human brain can stand the confusion.

SIR WALTER SCOTT.

Far ahint maun follow the faster.

Lord Lytton's Experience.

There is a time for everything.

A place for everything, and everything in its place.

SIR EDWARD BULWER LYTTON, before he was raised to the peerage as Lord Lytton, in a lecture which he delivered in a rural district in England, gave the following brief account of his literary habits; and the important lesson which it contains is sufficiently valuable to merit a place in our "Book of Good Devices."

Many persons seeing me so much engaged in active life, and as much about the world as if I had never been a student, have said to me, "When do you get time to write all your books? How do you contrive to do so much work?" I shall surprise you by the answer I made. I said, "I contrive to do so much by never doing too much at a time." A man, to get through work well, must not overwork himself; or, if he do too much to-day, the reaction of fatigue will come, and he will be obliged to do too little to-morrow. Now, since I began really and earnestly to study, which was not till I had left college, and was actually in the world, I may perhaps say that I have gone through as large a course of general reading as most men of my time. I have travelled much, and I have seen much; I have mixed much in politics, and in the various business of life; and, in addition to all this, I

Do one thing at a time.

have published somewhere about sixty volumes, some upon subjects requiring much special research. And what time do you think, as a general rule, I have devoted to study—to reading and writing? Not more than three hours a day; and, when Parliament is sitting, not always that. But then, during those hours, I have given my whole attention to what I was about.

An Idle Mind.

NO mind furnishes so inviting a field for the tempter as one that is unoccupied. No mind, no heart, save that of an idiot, can be wholly vacant or at rest. If not employed in that which is good, or at the least harmless, a troop of evil thoughts and passions come rushing in and take possession. How much of vice and ruinous dissipation has its origin in the fact that "time hangs heavy" on the idler's hand; and how many, in trying to kill time, in reality kill themselves! God pronounced more of a blessing than a curse in the decree, when He said, "In the sweat of thy brow shalt thou eat thy bread;" and in even compulsory toil He has furnished us with one of the grandest safeguards against temptation.

Slow to bed, slow to rise.

BE NOT SLOTHFUL IN BUSINESS.

THOSE violate this precept who have a lawful calling, a proper business, but are slothful in it. When people are in business for themselves, they are in less risk of transgressing this injunction; though even then it sometimes happens that the hand is not diligent enough to make its owner rich. But it is when engaged in business not for ourselves but for others, or for God, that we are in greatest danger of neglecting this rule. The servant who has no pleasure in his work, who does no more than wages can buy, or a legal agreement enforce, the shopman who does not enter *con amore* into his employer's interest, and bestir himself to extend his trade as he would strive were the concern his own; the scholar who trifles when his teacher's eye is elsewhere, and who is content if he can only learn enough to escape disgrace; the teacher who is satisfied if he can only impart a decent quantum of instruction, and who does not labour for the mental expansion and spiritual well-being of his pupils, as he would for those of his own children; the magistrate or civic functionary who is only careful to escape public censure, and who does not labour to make the community richer, or happier, or better for his administration; the minister who can give his

He is idle that might be better employed.

He is soon done that never begins.

Be not weary in well-doing.

Be not slothful in business.

energies to another cause than that of Christ, and neglect his Master's business in minding his own: every one, in short, who performs the work which God or his brethren have given him to do in a hireling and perfunctory manner, is a violator of the Divine injunction, "Not slothful in business." There are some persons of a dull and languid turn. They trail sluggishly through life, as if some painful viscus, some adhesive slime were clogging every movement, and making their snail-path a waste of their very substance. They do nothing with that healthy alacrity, that gleesome energy which bespeaks a sound mind even more than a vigorous body; but they drag themselves to the inevitable task with remonstrating reluctance, as if every joint were set in a socket of torture, or as if they expected the quick flesh to cleave to the next implement of industry they handled. Having no wholesome love of work, no joyous delight in duty, they do everything grudgingly, in the most superficial manner, and at the latest moment. Others there are who, if you find them at their post, you will find them dozing at it. They are a sort of perpetual somnambulists, walking through their sleep; moving in a constant mystery; looking for their faculties, and forgetting what they are looking for; not able to find their work, and when they have found their work not able to find their hands; doing everything dreamily, and there-

The Lord is far from the wicked.

Let not your good be evil spoken of.

Eye-servants are bad servants.

fore everything confusedly and incompletely; their work a dream, their sleep a dream, not repose, not refreshment, but a slumbrous vision of rest, a dreamy query concerning sleep; too late for everything; taking their passage when the ship has sailed, insuring their property when the house is burned, locking the door when the goods are stolen; men whose bodies seem to have started in the race of existence before their minds were ready, and who are always gazing out vacantly, as if they expected their wits coming up by the next arrival.

Such slothful dreamers are each and all of them unfaithful to their trust — "slothful in business." They betray the interests of all who have any connection with them, sacrifice the prospects of those who should be most dear to them, and frequently involve themselves in disgrace and ruin.

REV. JAMES HAMILTON.

STEADINESS OF PURPOSE.

STEADINESS of purpose overcomes difficulties—not with a rush and a shout, but one by one. They dissolve away before its incessant pressure, like icebergs before the steady radiance of the sun.

Steadiness of purpose gives a man the

strength of a happy conscience. A man who, like a weathercock, veers about with every breeze, cannot possess true quietness of mind. Self-dissatisfaction worries and annoys him; but a cheerful vigour and energy grows out of an intelligent, unviolating purpose. Steadiness of purpose gives dignity and honour to character. Men cannot but admire and respect the mind that marches on steadily through sunshine and shade, calm and storm, smiles and frowns; glad of favour, but pressing on without it; thankful for aid, but advancing nevertheless if it is not given; such men establish for themselves a character which secures both respect and honour.

Steadiness of purpose secures success. In any enterprise which is not impossible, a man with it must succeed. He has the chief element of triumph over every difficulty, and it will carry him through. He may not reach his goal at one bound, but he will gain it in the end. He moves not rapidly, but surely. When you want to find him, you will know when and where to look for him. If he has set out from the bottom of the ladder of life, he will be found to have successfully arrived at the top of it.

A virtuous woman is a crown to her husband.

On the Choice of a Wife.

WHEN it shall please God to bring thee to man's estate, use great providence and circumspection in choosing thy wife; for from thence will spring all thy future good or evil. And it is an action of thy life, like unto a stratagem of war, wherein a man can err but once. If thy estate be good, match near home and at leisure; if weak, far off and quickly. Inquire diligently of her disposition, and how her parents have been inclined in her youth. Let her not be poor, how well-born soever; for a man can buy nothing in the market with gentility. Nor choose a base and uncomely creature altogether for wealth; for it will cause contempt in others, and loathing in thee. Neither make choice of a dwarf or a fool; for thou shalt find it to thy great grief that there is nothing more fulsome than a she-fool.

And touching the guiding of thy house, let thy hospitality be moderate; and, according to the means of thy estate, rather plentiful than sparing, but not costly. For I never knew any man grow poor by keeping an orderly table. But some consume themselves through secret vices, and their hospitality bears the blame. But banish swinish drunkards out of thine house, which is a vice impairing health, con-

A good man makes a good wife.

suming much, and makes no show. I never heard praise ascribed to the drunkard, but the well-bearing his drink; which is a better commendation for a brewer's horse or a drayman, than for either a gentleman or a serving-man. Beware thou spend not above three or four parts of thy revenues; nor above a third part of that in thy house. For the other two parts will do no more than defray thy extraordinaries, which always surmount the ordinaries by much; otherwise thou shalt live, like a rich beggar, in continual want. And the needy man can never live happily nor contentedly; for every disaster makes him ready to mortgage or sell. And that gentleman who sells an acre of land, sells an ounce of credit. For gentility is nothing else but ancient riches. So that if the foundation shall at any time sink, the building must needs follow.

LORD BURLEIGH.

EVERY man ought to cultivate the habit of accurate and systematic reckoning in all pecuniary transactions. If they pertain to his own estates, business, or money transactions, it is a duty to himself and his family, on which their most important interests may be ultimately found to depend; and in so far as it involves the concerns or ultimate interests of others, it is a duty which no man can honestly dispense with.

There is no place like home.

LOVE OF COUNTRY.

THE first great duty of every citizen is that of an abiding love for his country. This is one of the native instincts of the noble heart. History tells of many a devoted hero, reared under an oppressive despotism, and groaning under unjust exactions, with little in the character of his ruler to excite anything like generous enthusiasm, who yet has shed his blood and given up his treasures in willing sacrifice for his country's good. In a country such as this we live in, it is the duty of every man to be a patriot, and to love and serve it with an affection that is commensurate both with the priceless cost of her liberties, and the greatness of her civil and religious privileges. Indeed, however it may be in other lands, in this one the youth may be said to draw in the love of country with his native air; and it is justly taken for granted that all will seek and maintain her interests, as that the child shall love its mother, on whose bosom it has been cradled, and of whose life it is a part.

In no other country more than this is it important that all should rightly understand and faithfully fulfil the duties of citizenship. While ignorance is the natural stronghold of tyranny, knowledge is the very throne of civil liberty. It is the interest of despotism

Forsake not the land of thy birth.

There is no land like the old land.

A rolling stone gathers no moss.

Good understanding getteth favour.

to foster a blind, unreasoning obedience to arbitrary law; but where, as with us, almost the humblest has a voice in the administration of public affairs, more depends upon the enlightened sentiments of the masses than upon even the skill of temporary rulers, or the character of existing laws.

EARL ST. VINCENT'S RESOLUTION.

MY father had a very large family, with limited means. He gave me twenty pounds at starting when I first went to sea as a midshipman, and that was all he ever gave me. After I had been a considerable time at the station I drew for twenty more, but the bill was not honoured. I was mortified at this rebuke, and made a promise, which I have ever kept, that I would never draw another bill without a certainty of its being paid. I immediately changed my mode of living, quitted my mess, lived alone, and took up the ship's allowance, which I found quite sufficient; washed and mended my own clothes; made a pair of trousers out of the ticking of my bed; and having by these means saved as much money as would redeem my honour, I took up my bill; and from that time I have taken care to keep within my means.

The evil bow before the good.

A wise man feareth, and departeth from evil.

The fool rageth, and is confident.

GOOD FOR EVIL.

GOOD for evil is the Bible law from first to last. It has been said very truly—"To render evil for good is devil-like; to render evil for evil is man-like; to render good for evil is God-like." The ungrateful forgetfulness of favours is bad, but the requital of good with evil is the very utmost stretch of depravity. Yet, alas! even this is far from being a rarity. Selfishness is the besetting sin of our fallen nature. It reigns paramount. It sets aside the claims of both God and man. Selfish men receive the good bestowed upon them merely for its own sake. They have no consideration for the giver further than as conveying the benefit to them. They feel no attachment on account of the principle by which the bestowment of it has been prompted, though to a generous spirit that is a gift's chief value. They snatch the good, and, in the enjoyment of it, never think more of the hand from which it came. What is that to them? Their own interest is promoted—and should the interest of the kind friend from whose bounty it has come ever stand in the way of theirs, they laugh at the thought of obligation, and sacrifice it without a scruple. "Every man for himself," is their base and sordid maxim.

O shun selfishness. Cultivate the generous and

Count money after all your kin.

forgiving spirit of the Bible: "Look not every man on his own things, but every man also on the things of others. Let *this* mind be in you, which was also in Christ Jesus."

DR. WARDLAW.

CAREFULNESS IN MONEY MATTERS.

PUNCTUALITY in money matters is one of the greatest sources of comfort and prosperity to the man of business—indeed, to every man. Punctuality in payment may be said to double our means. The man of disorderly habits, with no proper account of income and expenditure, and no just estimate of the relative proportion of his means and obligations, is perpetually exposed to the annoyance and vexation of having demands made upon him, not so much beyond his means, as disproportioned to the chance provisions of the moment. He may be compared to a general who, neglecting the discipline of his forces, may be surprised at any moment by the attack of the most insignificant foe, not because his numbers are insufficient, but because they are not at hand. The skilful commander, with but half the number, well disciplined, and ever ready at a moment's notice, is equal to almost any emergency.

Short accounts make long friends.

There is no friend like the penny.

Owe no man anything.

Swear not at all.

Profane Swearing.

PROFANE swearing is a most obnoxious vice, which is fearfully prevalent among the youth of the community. Even little boys, as we pass them in the street, startle us by their oaths. What is to be our condition, if this sin goes on undiminished and unrebuked? Our youth will come to such degradation that they will be unconscious of their profanity, and will, perhaps, deny that they are guilty of it altogether. But look at it—there is, to us, something terrifying in the thought that one whose breath is in his nostrils can call upon God to curse a mortal man, or the poor horse which he has overladen; or, perhaps, even the inanimate stumbling-block over which he falls.

What is there to justify this language? It is braving the very Being who created us, and in whose goodness we live; it is trampling the Bible under our feet; it is vulgar, ungentlemanly, and wicked. George Washington once heard an officer, when dining at his table, utter an oath. "I thought," said he, laying down his knife and fork, and speaking with peculiar dignity, "I thought we all supposed ourselves to be gentlemen." After dinner, the officer said to one of his companions, that if the general had

The tongue of the wise is health.

Take not the name of the Lord in vain.

An oath is the mark of a coward.

To swear is neither brave,

struck him over the head with his sword he could have borne it; but that home-thrust which he gave him was overpowering; it was "too much for a gentleman."

"What profit is there in this foul language?" said a young man. "I was profane when I was a boy." "And why did you leave it off?" he was asked. "Because," he replied, "it seemed to me to be useless." And, pray, what good can it possibly do to interlard a speech or conversation with profanity?

> "It chills my blood to hear the blest Supreme
> Rudely appealed to on each trifling theme.
> Maintain your rank; vulgarity despise—
> To swear is neither brave, polite, or wise."

Would you escape this low habit, I warn you to mark well when you are beginning to fall into its foul embrace. Avoid coarse, slang phrases; do not, on any occasion, deal in imprecations and protestations. Keep clear of half-oaths, and that border phraseology which carries you over, unaware, into the territory of open profanity. Reverence always the name of God, and be slow to pronounce it at any time; let every subject, person, and place that is sacred receive your respect. No one, with any true honour for God or for man, will defile his lips by uttering an oath.

Polite, or wise.

THE VALUE OF SYSTEM.

THE professional man places the highest value upon system. However clever, ingenious, or fruitful in expedients a youth may be, if he is erratic and disorderly in his personal or mental habits, he is thereby unfitted for many kinds of work. The plodding and methodical youth will outstrip him, and leave him behind; and this not merely in the more mechanical professions, but to a great extent also in the more intellectual professions. Life itself, with all its free and happy outgoings, is systematic. Order reigns everywhere; and in no business of life can this great principle be neglected with impunity. Even on those who seem to obey it least, externally, it operates; the very force that sustains them, and which, in its apparently irregular action, might seem to be defiant of all law, is only preserved at all by some enveloping although undefined order.

The young must keep before them this necessity of all business. They may hear it sometimes spoken of among their fellows with indifference and scorn. "Red tape" has passed into a byword of contempt; and "red tape," in the sense of a mere dead and unintelligent routine, has deserved many hard things to be said of it. A man of routine and nothing else

Safe bind, safe find.

is a poor creature. System which ceases to be a means, and becomes in itself—apart from the very object for which it was originally designed—an end, proves itself, in this very fact, a nuisance to be swept away, the sooner the better. But the abuse of a thing is no argument against its use, and it is childish not to see this in any case. Routine in and for itself has no value; and the mind that settles on the mere outside of work, forgetful of its inner meaning and real aim, is necessarily a mind of feeble and narrow energies; but routine, as an organ of energetic thought and action—of a living, comprehensive intelligence, which sees the end from the means—is one of the most powerful instruments of human accomplishment; and there can be no profession without its appropriate and effective routine.

Let every youthful aspirant carefully learn the letter without forgetting the spirit of his profession. Let him subdue his energies to his system, but not allow his system to swallow up his energies. Let him be a man of routine, but let him be something more. Let him be master of its machinery, but capable of rising above it. With the former he cannot dispense; without the latter he cannot be great or successful.

PRINCIPAL TULLOCH.

A good watch prevents harm.

PECUNIARY EMBARRASSMENT.

THERE is, perhaps, nothing which so grinds the human soul, and produces such an insupportable burden of wretchedness and despondency, as pecuniary pressure. Nothing more frequently drives men to suicide; and there is, perhaps, no danger to which men in an active and enterprising community are more exposed. Almost all are eagerly reaching forward to a station in life a little above what they can well afford, or struggling to do a business a little more extensive than they have capital or steady credit for; and thus they keep, all through life, just above their means—and *just above*, no matter by how small an excess, is inevitable misery.

Be sure then, if your aim is happiness, to bring down, at all hazards, your style of living, and your responsibilities of business, to such a point that you shall easily be able to reach it. Do this, I say, at all hazards. If you cannot have money enough for your purpose in a house with two rooms, take a house with one. It is your only chance for happiness. For there is such a thing as happiness in a single room, with plain furniture, and simple fare; but there is no such thing as happiness with responsibilities which cannot be met, and debts increasing without any

"I am the light of the world."

prospect of their discharge. If your object is gentility, or the credit of belonging to good society, or the most rapid accumulation of property, and you are willing to sacrifice happiness for it, I might, perhaps, give you different advice; but if your real object is to secure happiness, this is the only way.

JACOB ABBOTT.

THE GREAT EXEMPLAR.

CHRIST was an example to men of all classes and under every variety of circumstances. To the great? "A greater than Solomon is here." To the mean? "Is not this the carpenter?" To the rich? He is "heir of all things." To the poor? "Foxes have holes, and the birds of the air have nests; but the Son of man hath not where to lay his head." To the famous? "Behold the world is gone after him!" To the obscure? "Can there any good thing come out of Nazareth?" To the sorrowing? "Jesus wept." To the joyous? He "rejoiced in spirit." To the tempted? "All these things will I give thee if thou wilt fall down and worship me." To the injured? "His visage was marred more than any man, and his form more than the sons of men." To the powerful?

The name of the Lord is a strong tower.

Be ye kind one to another,

Tender-hearted one to another.

Righteousness tendeth to life.

"Thinkest thou that I cannot now pray to my Father, and he shall presently give me more than twelve legions of angels?" To the loved? "Lord, I am ready to go with thee to prison and to death." To the slighted? "I know not the man." To the insulted? "Be ye come out as against a thief with swords and with staves?" To the betrayed? "Whomsoever I shall kiss, that same is he; take him, and lead him away safely." To the idol of the crowd? "Hosanna to the Son of David!" To the butt of their scorn? "Away with this man, and release unto us Barabbas!"
REV. O. G. CAMPBELL.

TRUE NOBILITY.

NOBILITY of blood
Is but a glitt'ring and fallacious good.
The Nobleman is he whose noble mind   [kind.
Is fill'd with inbred worth, unborrowed from his
Virtue alone is true nobility:
Let your own acts immortalise your name,
'Tis poor relying on another's fame:
For take the pillars but away, and all
The superstructure must in ruins fall;
As a vine droops, when by divorce removed
From the embraces of the elm she lov'd.
DRYDEN.

Let the peace of God rule in your hearts.

Righteousness keepeth him that is upright.

By pride cometh contention.

Know thyself.

BE WHAT YOU SEEM.

NEVER affect to be other than you really are —either richer or wiser. Never be ashamed to say, "I do not know." Men will then believe you when you say, "I do know." Never be ashamed to say, whether as applied to time or money, "I cannot afford it. I cannot afford to waste a day in the idleness to which you invite me, or to spend a sovereign in the way you wish me." Once establish yourself and your mode of life as what they really are, and your feet are on solid ground, whether for the gradual step onward, or for the sudden seizure of a favourable opportunity. Learn to say "No" with decision, "Yes" with caution—"No" with decision when it meets a temptation, "Yes" with caution when it implies a promise. A promise once given should be regarded as a bond inviolable. A man is already of consequence in the world when it is known that he may be implicitly relied upon. We frequently see, in everyday life, persons preferred from a long list of applicants for some important post, which exalts them at once in station and fortune, merely because they have the reputation of being men of their word —men who, when they say that they know a thing, really know it, and when they say they will do a thing, will really perform it.

Seem what you are.

The mouth of the foolish is a rod of pride.

Every prudent man dealeth with knowledge.

The Danger of Speculation.

MONEY itself is good. In the words of Solomon, "it answereth all things;" not only luxury, but comfort, convenience, necessity demand it. And yet the acquisition of it is beset with moral perils. In our insane eagerness to be rich we delude ourselves with the idea that gold can fill and satisfy the soul. We regard no calamity so great as pecuniary want. The boy has his money-box, and learns to hoard as soon as he can speak. "The chief end of man," he is taught, is to make a good bargain. He is fired with a passion to set up in business for himself prematurely, and to rush into every path that seems to open out into a boundless accumulation.

Two tempters stand before the young man, and beckon him to follow them. First, a reckless speculation. Under this influence men are ready to invest their all in projects, a few of which may be likely or profitable, but the greater portion of which are visionary and chimerical. Bales of goods and risks of commission are staked at the table; and even many kinds of business, once followed with honesty, moderation, and a healthy success, are now pursued as games of chance.

Not a few thus spread out their business till it gets beyond their control; they overbuy goods; they live beyond their means, trusting that everything will come right in the end. So eager are they for all possible investments that, as a man said, "If it were proposed to build a bridge to Tophet, the stock would readily be taken up." But soon every mercantile building so founded totters and falls, and great is its fall.

Others, in their passion for sudden accumulation, practise secret frauds, and imagine there is no harm in it so long as they are not detected. But they cover up their transgression in vain—God sees it to the bottom; and let them not hope to keep it always even from man. In the long chain of events, "be sure your sin will find you out." He who is carrying on a course of latent corruption and dishonesty—be he president of some mammoth corporation, head of a manufacturing establishment, or engaged only in a small private business—is sailing in a ship, like that fabled one of old, which comes ever nearer and nearer to the magnetic mountain, that will at last draw every nail out of it. All faith in God and all trust in man will eventually be lost, and he will get not reward but punishment for his guilt. The very winds will sigh forth his iniquity; and "a beam will come out of the wall" to convict and smite him.

Better the noble resolution of Franklin. "My years roll round," said he, writing to his mother, "and the last will come, when I had rather have it said 'He lived usefully,' than 'He died rich.'"

THOROUGHNESS IN STUDY.

THOROUGHNESS and accuracy are two principal points to be aimed at in study. Francis Horner, in laying down rules for the cultivation of his mind and character, placed great stress upon the habit of continuous application to one subject for the sake of mastering it thoroughly; confining himself, with this object, to but a few books, and resisting with the greatest firmness "every approach to desultory reading." The value of knowledge to any man certainly consists not in its quantity, but mainly in the good uses to which he may apply it. Hence a little knowledge, of an exact and perfect character, is always found more valuable for practical purposes than any extent of superficial learning. The phrase in common use, as to "the *spread* of knowledge," is no doubt correct, but it is spread so widely, and in such thin layers, that it only serves to reveal the mass of ignorance lying underneath. Never, perhaps, were books more extensively read, or less studied; and the number is rapidly increasing of those who know a little of everything, but nothing well. Such readers have not inaptly been likened to a certain sort of pocket-knife which some people carry about with them, which, in addition to a common knife, contains a file, a chisel, a saw, a gimlet, a screw-driver, and a pair of scissors; but all so diminutive, that the moment they are needed for use, they are found useless.

One of Ignatius Loyola's maxims was, "He who does well one work at a time, does more than all." By spreading our efforts over too large a surface we inevitably weaken our force, hinder our progress, and acquire a habit of fitfulness and ineffective working. Whatever a youth undertakes to learn, he should not be suffered to leave it until he can reach his arms round it and clench his hands on the other side. Thus he will learn the habit of thoroughness. Lord St. Leonards once communicated to Sir Fowell Buxton the mode in which he had conducted his studies, and thus explained the secret of his success. "I resolved," said he, "when beginning to read law, to make everything I acquired perfectly my own, and never to go to a second thing till I had entirely accomplished the first. Many of my competitors read as much in a day as I read in a week; but, at the end of twelve months, my knowledge was as fresh as the day it was acquired, while theirs had glided away from recollection." SAMUEL SMILES.

Do that which is right—

EVERYDAY COURAGE.

THE greater part of the courage that is needed in the world is not of a heroic kind. Courage may be displayed in everyday life as well as in historic fields of action. There needs, for example, the common courage to be honest—the courage to resist temptation—the courage to speak the truth—the courage to be what we really are, and not to pretend to be what we are not—the courage to live honestly within our own means, and not dishonestly upon the means of others.

A great deal of the unhappiness, and much of the vice, of the world is owing to weakness and indecision of purpose—in other words, to lack of courage. Men may know what is right, and yet fail to exercise the courage to do it; they may understand the duty they have to do, but will not summon up the requisite resolution to perform it. The weak and undisciplined man is at the mercy of every temptation; he cannot say "No," but falls before it. And if his companionship be bad, he will be all the easier led away by bad example into wrong-doing.

Nothing can be more certain than that the character can only be sustained and strengthened by its own energetic action. The will, which is the central

Where there's a will there's a way.

Evil never came from good advice.

The respect of men will follow after.

Look before you leap.

force of character, must be trained to habits of decision—otherwise it will neither be able to resist evil nor to follow good. Decision gives the power of standing firmly, when to yield, however slightly, might be only the first step in a downhill course to ruin.

Calling upon others for help in forming a decision is worse than useless. A man must so train his habits as to rely upon his own powers and depend upon his own courage in moments of emergency. Plutarch tells of a King of Macedon who, in the midst of an action, withdrew into the adjoining town under pretence of sacrificing to Hercules; whilst his opponent Emilius, at the same time that he implored the Divine aid, sought for victory sword in hand, and won the battle. And so it ever is in the actions of daily life.

Many are the valiant purposes formed, that end merely in words; deeds intended, that are never done; designs projected, that are never begun; and all for want of a little courageous decision. Better far the silent tongue but the eloquent deed. For in life, and in business, dispatch is better than discourse; and the shortest of all is *Doing*. "In matters of great concern, and which must be done," says Tillotson, "there is no surer argument of a weak mind than irresolution—to be undetermined when the case is so plain and the necessity so urgent. To be always intending to live

Strike the iron while 'tis hot.

A good name is easier lost than won.

Better sit still than rise and fall.

Books are true friends,

a new life, but never to find time to set about it—this is as if a man should put off eating and drinking and sleeping from one day to another, until he is starved and destroyed."

SAMUEL SMILES.

The Companionship of Books.

LITERARY taste, apart from its higher uses, is among the most pure and enduring of earthly enjoyments. It brings its possessor into ever-renewing communion with all that is highest and best in the thought and sentiment of the past. The garnered wisdom of the ancient is its daily food. Whatever is dignified or lofty in speculation, or refined or elevated in feeling, or wise, quaint, or humorous in suggestion, or soaring or tender in imagination, is accessible to the lover of books. He can command the wittiest or wisest of companions at his pleasure. He can retire and hold converse with philosophers, statesmen, and poets; he can regale himself with their richest and deepest thoughts, with their most exquisite felicities of expression. His favourite books are a world to him. He lives with their characters; he is animated by their sentiments; he is moved by their principles.

That will neither flatter nor dissemble.

Books should to one of these four ends conduce—Wisdom, piety, delight, or use.

A good book is a true friend.

And when the outer world is a burden to him—when its ambitions fret him, or its cares worry him—he finds refuge in this calmer world of the past, and soothes his resentment and stimulates his languor in peaceful sympathy with it.

Especially does this love of literature rise into enjoyment, when other and more active enjoyments begin to fade away. When the senses lose their freshness, and the limbs their activity, the man who has learned to love books has a constant and ever-growing interest. When the summit of professional life has been attained, and wealth secured, and the excitements of business yield to the desire for retirement, such a man has a happy resource in himself; and the taste which he cultivated at intervals, and sometimes almost by stealth, amid the pressure of business avocations, becomes to him at once an ornament and a blessing. It is impossible to overrate the comparative dignity, as well as enjoyment, of a life thus well spent, which has preserved an intellectual feeling amidst commercial ventures or sordid distractions, and brightens at last into evening of intellectual wisdom and calm.

PRINCIPAL TULLOCH.

No entertainment is so cheap as reading.

The tongue of the wise useth knowledge aright.

Reading maketh a full man.

Too soon is easy mended.

THE UNPUNCTUAL MAN

Good understanding getteth favour.

THE unpunctual man is a general disturber of others' peace and serenity. Everybody with whom he has to do is thrown from time to time into a state of fever; he is systematically late: regular only in his irregularity. He conducts his dawdling as if upon a system; always arrives at his appointment after time; gets to the railway station after the train has started; and posts his letters when the box has closed. Business is thus thrown into confusion, and everybody concerned is put out of temper. It will generally be found that the men who are thus habitually behind time are as habitually behind success; and the world generally casts them aside to swell the ranks of the grumblers and the railers against fortune. The late Thomas Tegg, the publisher, who rose from a very humble position in life, once said of himself that he "had lodged with beggars, and had the honour of presentation to royalty," and that he attributed his success in life mainly to three things—punctuality as to time, self-reliance, and integrity in word and deed. The miscalculation of time involves us in perpetual hurry, confusion, and difficulties; and life becomes a mere shuffle of expedients, usually followed by

Better late thrive than never do well.

Always in a hurry is ever behind.

disaster. Lord Nelson said, "I owe all my success in life to having been always a quarter of an hour before my time."   SAMUEL SMILES.

THE INFLUENCE OF READING.

A MAN'S reading is usually a fair index of his character. Observe, in almost any house you visit, the books which lie customarily on the parlour table, or note what are brought home for perusal from the library, and you may form a pretty accurate idea, not only of the intellectual tastes and the general intelligence of the members of the family, but also, and what is of deeper moment, of the moral attainments and spiritual advancement of the household. "A man is known," it is said, "by the company he keeps." It is equally true that a man's character may be, to a great extent, ascertained by knowing what books he reads. A bad book cannot be read without leaving a baneful influence behind it; and it is almost impossible to peruse a good book without feeling the better for it. Bad books are like ardent spirits—both intoxicate, one the mind, the other the body; and the thirst for each increases by being indulged, and is never satisfied. Both ruin, one the intellect, the other the health, and both the soul. Precious, on the other hand, and priceless, are the blessings that good books scatter in our daily path. They bring us into the society of the good, noblest, and truest men of all ages and countries, and carry us into the fairest regions of earth, at our own free will.

"Not to know what was before you were, is," as has been truly said, "to be always a child." And it is equally true that he never becomes a complete man who learns nothing of the former days from reading. "Books," says a good writer, "are the crystalline founts which hold, in eternal ice, the imperishable gems of the past."

BE OF GOOD COURAGE.

GOOD courage is the salt of character. Some, because they have failed in their undertakings once or twice, or meet with a rebuff, become discouraged, and sink into despair and inactivity. Such should know that our own errors may often teach us more than the grave precepts of others. Let us counsel the young man never to despair. If he can make nothing by any work that presents itself now, he can at least make

Never despair.

himself; or, what is equivalent, he can save himself from the sure death of a pusillanimous, irresolute, halting spirit. Never be cast down by misfortunes. If a spider break his web, over and over he will mend it again; and do not you therefore fall behind the very insect on your walls. If the sun is going down, look up to the stars; if earth is dark, keep your eye on heaven. With the presence and promise of God, we can bear up under anything, and should press on, never halting, never fearing.

Never lose faith in God or His goodness. If we once lose that, we become irreligious, living not for the eye of our Father above, but for the mere favour of man. Hence, too, our young men, sometimes cherishing doubts of the soul and immortality, live for the body alone, and plunge into sensuality and wickedness, votaries of animal appetite and of sin. Let one yield to this sceptical feeling, and he will respect talent before virtue, and fall down and worship the man of great intellect, however destitute of principle. A Cæsar then stands in his scale higher than a Fénelon. Let a man make a splendid oration, and though his character be scarred over, as Herod's was, with deeds of rapine and carnage, the shout goes up, "It is the voice of a god, and not of a man: let us worship the earthly god rather than the Heavenly King!"

If at first you don't succeed, *Try, try, try again.*

Courage is the salt of character.

An honest man's the noblest work of God.

Habits of a Man of Business.

A SACRED regard to the principles of justice ought to form the basis of every commercial transaction, and regulate the conduct of the upright man of business.

He is strict in keeping his engagements.

He does nothing carelessly, or in a hurry.

He employs no person to do for him what he can do for himself.

He keeps everything in its proper place, and does everything at its proper time.

He leaves nothing undone that ought to be done, and which circumstances permit him to do.

He keeps his designs and business from the knowledge of others.

He is prompt, decisive, civil and obliging to his customers.

He does not overtrade his capital.

He prefers cash to credit; but if credit is necessary, as short a time as possible.

He prefers small profits and certain returns to large profits and uncertain settlements.

He is clear and explicit in making a bargain.

He leaves nothing of consequence to memory which he can commit to writing.

Civilities cost nothing.

He that oppresseth the poor reproacheth his Maker.

A tale-bearer revealeth secrets.

In all labour there is profit.

He that speaketh truth sheweth forth righteousness.

He that is slow to wrath is of great understanding.

He keeps copies of all important letters written by him, and carefully preserves all which he receives.

He is methodical in his habits and arrangements.

He is always at the head of his business.

He holds it as an axiom, that he whose credit is doubted should not be trusted.

He constantly examines his books, and sees that they are properly kept.

He makes a balance of the true state of his affairs at regular intervals.

He avoids lawsuits and accommodation bills.

He is economical in his expenditure, and lives within his income.

He is cautious in becoming security for any person.

He is generous, but not until he has been just.

Let a man of business conform strictly to these habits; when once formed they are easily retained, and success will result from their practice.

Let him take pleasure in his business, and it will become a recreation to him.

Let him hope for the best, be prepared for the worst, and bear resolutely whatever happens.

REAL glory
Springs from the silent conquest of ourselves,
And without that the conqueror is not
But the first slave.

Be not above thy business.

The Deceit of the Heart.

EPICTETUS tells us of a gentleman returning from banishment, who, in his journey towards home, called at his house, told a sad story of an imprudent life, the greatest part of which being now spent, he was resolved for the future to live philosophically and entertain no business, to be candidate for no employment, not to go to the court, not to salute Cæsar with ambitious attendances, but to study, and worship the gods, and die willingly when nature and necessity called him. It may be this man believed himself, but Epictetus did not; and he had reason. Letters from Cæsar met him at the doors, and invited him to court; and he forgot all his promises which were warm upon his lips, and grew pompous, secular, and ambitious, and gave the gods thanks for his preferment. Thus many men leave the world when their fortune hath left them; and they are severe and philosophical, and retired for ever, if for ever it be impossible to return. But let a prosperous sunshine warm and refresh their sadnesses, and make it but possible to break their purposes, and there needs no more temptation; their own false heart is enough; they are like Ephraim in the day of battle, starting aside like a broken bough.

The heart is false, deceiving and deceived, in its

intentions and designs. A man hears the precepts of God enjoining us to give alms of all we possess; he readily obeys with much cheerfulness and alacrity, and his charity, like a fair-spreading tree, looks beauteously. But there is a canker at the heart; the man blows a trumpet to call the poor together, and hopes the neighbourhood will take notice of his bounty. Nay, he gives alms privately, and charges no man to speak of it, and yet hopes by some accident or other to be praised both for his charity and humility. And if, by chance, the fame of his alms come abroad, it is but his duty to "let his light so shine before men" that God may be glorified.   JEREMY TAYLOR.

YOUTHFUL ENERGY.

HOW precious a thing is youthful energy, if only it could be preserved entirely englobed as it were within the bosom of the young adventurer, till he can come and offer it forth a sacred emanation in yonder temple of truth and virtue; but, alas! all along as he goes towards it, he advances through an avenue formed by a long line of tempters and demons on each side, all prompt to touch him with their conductors, and draw this divine electric element with which he is charged, away.
JOHN FOSTER.

How Cobbett Learned Grammar.

I LEARNED grammar when I was a private soldier, on the pay of sixpence a day. The edge of my berth, or that of my guard-bed, was my seat to study in; my knapsack was my bookcase; a bit of board, lying on my lap, was my writing-table; and the task did not demand anything like a year of my life. I had no money to purchase candle or oil; in winter time it was rarely that I could get any evening light but that of the fire, and only my turn even of that. And if I, under such circumstances, and without parent or friend to advise or encourage me, accomplished this undertaking, what excuse can there be for any youth, however poor, however pressed with business, or however circumstanced as to room or other conveniences? To buy a pen or a sheet of paper I was compelled to forego some portion of food, though in a state of half-starvation. I had no moment of time that I could call my own; and I had to read and to write amidst the talking, laughing, singing, whistling, and brawling of at least half a score of the most thoughtless of men, and that, too, in the hours of their freedom from all control. Think not lightly of the farthing that I had to give, now and then, for pen, ink, or paper! That farthing was, alas! a great sum to

To the willing all things are possible.

me! I was as tall as I am now; I had great health and great exercise. The whole of the money not expended for us at market was twopence a week for each man. I remember, and well I may, that on one occasion I, after all necessary expenses, had, on a Friday, made shifts to have a halfpenny in reserve, which I had destined for the purchase of a red herring in the morning; but when I pulled off my clothes at night, so hungry then as to be hardly able to endure life, I found that I had lost my halfpenny! I buried my head under the miserable sheet and rug, and cried like a child! And again I say, if I, under circumstances like these, could encounter and overcome this task, is there, can there be, in the whole world, a youth to find an excuse for the non-performance?

HABIT.

IF you plant the seed and nourish it, it would be as easy to check the growth of a forest, as to stop its progress to confirmed and sturdy habit. Habits are growing very fast, and soon close like the ices on the opposite shores of the arctic seas, except dashed by the interruption of a mighty force. Is the spectator unconcerned while they are closing around him? perhaps descanting wisely on the laws of habit while he is becoming its victim. JOHN FOSTER.

A good man leaveth an inheritance

To his children's children.

Do what you ought, come what will.

Work while it is called to-day,

The First Condition of Success.

THE first condition of success in every profession, is earnest devotion to its requirements and duties. This may seem so obvious a remark that it is scarcely worth making. And yet, with all its obviousness, the thing itself is often forgotten by the young. They are frequently loth to admit the extent and urgency of professional claims; and they try to combine with these claims devotion to some favourite and, even it may be, conflicting pursuit. This almost invariably fails. In rare cases it may be practicable with men of varied and remarkable powers, but ordinarily there is no chance of success in professional life for any who do not make the business of their profession, whatever it may be, their great interest, to which every other, save religion, must subordinate itself.

"Whatsoever thy hand findeth to do, do it with thy might," is the motto of all industrial activity. In such a time as ours it is so more than ever. If we do not do our work with might, others will; and they will outstrip us in the race, and pluck the prize from our grasp. "The race is not always to the swift, nor the battle to the strong," says the same wise man, and this is true in various forms and illustrations; but

Success is only obtained by perseverance.

Do ill, doubt all; do well, doubt none.

For the night cometh, when no man can work.

The present time's our own,

scarcely ever in the race of business, or in the battle of industrial life: there the swiftest wins the prize, and the strongest gains in the strife.
PRINCIPAL TULLOCH.

OPPORTUNITY EVERYTHING.

THE most ordinary occasions will furnish a man with opportunities or suggestions for improvement, if he be but prompt to take advantage of them. Professor Lee was first attracted to the study of Hebrew by finding a Bible in this language in a synagogue, while working as a common carpenter at the repairs of the benches. He became possessed with a desire to read the book in the original, and, buying a cheap second-hand copy of a Hebrew grammar, he set to work, and soon learnt the language for himself. As Edmund Stone said to the Duke of Argyll, in answer to the inquiries of his Grace, how he, a poor gardener's boy, had contrived to be able to read "Newton's Principia" in Latin—"One needs only to know the twenty-four letters of the alphabet in order to learn everything that one wishes." Application and perseverance, and the diligent improvement of opportunities, will do the rest. SAMUEL SMILES.

The future none can see.

Make hay while the sun shines.

Take time ere time is lost.

Time flies.

THE VALUE OF TIME.

WHATEVER we have to do should be done at the right time. To the busy man there is nothing more valuable than time. Every hour and every moment becomes filled up with its appointed duties; and attention to these duties at the moment when they fall to be performed is of the very essence of a business character. It is marvellous how comparatively easy the discharge of business becomes when this simple rule is observed, and how difficult and complicated it becomes when it is disregarded. It may be safely said that no man can rise to distinction as a merchant, a barrister, or a physician, or indeed in any profession involving a complexity of work, without a strict observance of punctuality. In some professions it may not be customary to exact or expect the same regard to this rule; but this is entirely without any warrant in reason, or the nature of the duties to which the indulgence may be applied. For it is impossible to conceive any duties, not absolutely accidental, beyond the rule of punctuality. Touch them with this rule, and they will fall into order; leave them independent of it, and inextricable confusion will be the result. . . .

It may seem an easy thing to be punctual, but it

A day to come seems longer than a year that's gone.

An hour in the morning is worth two at night.

Time once lost can never be recalled.

Punctuality is the soul of business.

is not an easy thing. It does not come to us naturally. No habits of order do, as may be observed in the utter disorder that characterises savage life, and low and untutored forms of life among ourselves. Punctuality is something we have all to learn; and of every profession—of all work—it is one of the first lessons; a lesson not only indispensable to ourselves, but due to others. How much so, every one knows who has to do with the unpunctual man. All is deranged by him: the time of others is deranged by him: the time of others is wasted as well as his own. He becomes a nuisance in society; and men who have real work of their own would rather do anything than do business with him.

Every young man, therefore, should acquire punctuality among his first professional achievements. Let him resolve to keep time—to do everything in its place. Let him not yield to the delusion, common enough among the young, that this is an unimportant matter, in the power of any man, and which he can practise when he has more real need for it than as yet he has. Vain expectation! If he begins by neglecting it, he will most assuredly end by neglecting it. Nothing is so hard *to unlearn* as a bad habit of this kind. It cleaves to the will even after the reason may strongly recognise its selfishness and inconvenience.

PRINCIPAL TULLOCH.

Order is heaven's first law.

There is a time for everything.

"Now" is the best watchword.

The desire of wisdom

Carlyle's Advice to Young Men.

THE following admirable letter by Thomas Carlyle, Esq., was addressed to a young man who had written to him desiring his advice as to a proper choice of reading, and, it would appear also, as to his conduct in general. We earnestly recommend it to the attention of our readers, as containing advice of the most valuable and practical description, and pregnant with truths with which they cannot be too well acquainted. The young are too much inclined to be dissatisfied with their actual condition, and to neglect their immediate duties in vain aspirations after others beyond their lot; and they need the monitions of such a kind but vigorous and emphatic adviser as Mr. Carlyle, and to have it impressed upon their minds that

"To do
That which before us lies in daily life
Is the prime wisdom."

"Dear Sir,—Some time ago your letter was delivered me; I take literally the first free half-hour I have had since to write you a word of answer.

"It would give me true satisfaction could any advice of mine contribute to forward you in your honourable course of self-improvement, but a long experience has taught me

The multitude of the wise

Is the welfare of the world.

Bringeth to a kingdom.

that advice can profit but little; that there is a good reason why advice is so seldom followed—this reason namely, that it is so seldom, and can almost never be, rightly given. No man knows the state of another; it is always to some more or less imaginary man that the wisest and most honest adviser is speaking.

"As to the books which you—whom I know so little of—should read, there is hardly anything definite that can be said. For one thing, you may be strenuously advised to keep reading. Any good book, any book that is wiser than yourself, will teach you something—a great many things, indirectly and directly, if your mind be open to learn. This old counsel of Johnson's is also good, and universally applicable:—'Read the book you do honestly feel a wish and curiosity to read.' The very wish and curiosity indicates that you, then and there, are the person likely to get good of it. 'Our wishes are presentiments of our capabilities;' that is a noble saying, of deep encouragement to all true men; applicable to our wishes and efforts in regard to reading as to other things. Among all the objects that look wonderful or beautiful to you, follow with fresh hope the one which looks wonderfullest, beautifullest. You will gradually find, by various trials (which trials see that you make honest, manful ones, not silly, short, fitful ones), what *is* for you the wonderfullest, beautifullest—what is *your* true element and province, and be able to profit by that. True desire, the monition of nature, is much to be attended to. But here, also, you are to discriminate carefully between *true* desire and false. The medical men tell us we should eat what we *truly* have an appetite for; but what we only *falsely* have an appetite for we should resolutely avoid. It is very true; and flimsy, desultory readers, who fly from

Good advice is never out of season.

foolish book to foolish book, and get good of none, and mischief of all—are not these as foolish, unhealthy eaters, who mistake their superficial false desire after spiceries and confectioneries for their real appetite, of which even they are not destitute, though it lies far deeper, far quieter, after solid nutritive food? With these illustrations, I will recommend Johnson's advice to you.

"Another thing, and only one other, I will say. All books are properly the record of the history of past men—what thoughts past men had in them—what actions past men did: the summary of all books whatsoever lies there. It is on this ground that the class of books specifically named History can be safely recommended as the basis of all study of books—the preliminary to all right and full understanding of anything we can expect to find in books. Past history, and especially the past history of one's own native country, everybody may be advised to begin with that. Let him study that faithfully; innumerable inquiries will branch out from it; he has a broad-beaten highway, from which all the country is more or less visible; there travelling, let him choose where he will dwell.

"Neither let mistakes and wrong directions—of which every man, in his studies and elsewhere, falls into many—discourage you. There is precious instruction to be got by finding that we are wrong. Let a man try faithfully, manfully, to be right, he will grow daily more and more right. It is, at bottom, the condition on which all men have to cultivate themselves. Our very walking is an incessant falling—a falling and a catching of ourselves before we come actually to the pavement!—it is emblematic of all things a man does.

"In conclusion, I will remind you that it is not by books

Study the history of your own country.

Faithfully endeavour to do right.

Good counsel is above price.

Glorious is the fruit of good works.

alone, or by books chiefly, that a man becomes in all points a man. Study to do faithfully whatsoever thing in your actual situation, there and now, you find either expressly or tacitly laid to your charge; that is your post; stand in it like a true soldier. Silently devour the many chagrins of it, as all human situations have many; and see you aim not to quit it without doing all that *it*, at least, required of you. A man perfects himself by work much more than by reading. They are a growing kind of men that can wisely combine the two things—wisely, valiantly, can do what is laid to their hand in their present sphere, and prepare themselves withal for doing other wider things, if such lie before them.

"With many good wishes and encouragements, I remain, yours sincerely,

"THOMAS CARLYLE.

"CHELSEA, 13*th March*, 1843."

Let us walk honestly, as in the day.

Bear ye one another's burdens.

THE FOUNDATION OF MERCANTILE CHARACTER.

FAITH and trustfulness lie at the foundation of trade and commercial intercourse, and business transactions of every kind. A community of known swindlers and knaves would try in vain to avail themselves of the advantages of traffic, or to gain access to those circles where honour and honesty are indispensable passports. Hence the value which is attached, by all right-minded men, to purity of purpose and integrity of character. A man may be unfortunate, he may be poor and penniless; but if he is known to possess unbending integrity, an unwavering purpose to do what is honest and just, he will have friends and patrons whatever may be the embarrassments and exigencies into which he is thrown. The poor man may thus possess a capital of which none of the misfortunes and calamities of life can deprive him. We have known men who have been suddenly reduced from affluence to penury by misfortunes, which they could neither foresee nor prevent. A fire has swept away the accumulations of years; misplaced confidence, a flood, or some of the thousand casualties to which commercial men are exposed, have stripped them of their possessions. To-day they have been

Let none of you suffer as an evil-doer.

Abstain from all appearance of evil.

A safe conscience makes a sound sleep.

Roguery means ruin:

prosperous, to-morrow every prospect is blighted, and everything in its aspect is dark and dismal. Their business is gone, their property is gone, and they feel that all is gone; but they have a rich treasure which the fire cannot consume, which the flood cannot carry away. They have integrity of character, and this gives them influence, raises up friends, and furnishes them with means to start afresh in the world once more. Young men, especially, should be deeply impressed with the vast importance of cherishing those principles, and of cultivating those habits, which will secure for them the confidence and esteem of the wise and good. Let it be borne in mind that no brilliancy of genius, no tact or talent in business, and no amount of success, will compensate for duplicity, shuffling, and trickery. There may be apparent advantage in the art and practice of dissimulation, and in violating those great principles which lie at the foundation of truth and duty; but it will at length be seen that a pound was lost where a penny was gained; that present successes are outweighed, a thousandfold, by the pains and penalties which result from loss of confidence and loss of reputation. It cannot be too strongly impressed upon the minds of young men to abstain from every course, from every act, which shocks their moral sensibilities, wounds their conscience, and has a tendency to weaken that nice sense of honour and integrity so

Enter not into the path of the wicked,

And go not in the way of evil men.

Integrity means success.

indispensable to character. The habit of concealment, of dissimulation, of telling "white lies," as they have been called, is most disastrous in all its influences and issues. How many have become confirmed liars, and been consigned to dishonour and infamy, who began their career in this way! Language is utterly inadequate to describe the amazing, the infinite importance to young men, of forming their characters from right models, and in accordance with the unchanging principles of truth.

BUSINESS.

BUSINESS is the salt of life, which not only gives a grateful smack to it, but dries up those crudities that would offend, preserves from putrefaction, and drives off all those blowing flies that would corrupt it. Let a man be sure to drive his business rather than let it drive him. When a man is but once brought to be driven, he becomes a vassal to his affairs. Reason and right give the quickest dispatch. All the entanglements that we meet with arise from the irrationality of ourselves or others. With a wise and honest man a business is soon ended, but with a fool and knave there is no conclusion, and seldom even a beginning.

The righteous are bold as a lion.

KEEP GOOD COMPANY.

IT is a common saying that men are known by the company they keep. The sober do not associate with the drunken, the refined with the coarse, the decent with the dissolute. To associate with depraved persons argues a low taste and vicious tendencies, and to frequent their society leads to inevitable degradation of character. "The conversation of such persons," says Seneca, "is very injurious; for even if it does no immediate harm, it leaves its seeds in the mind, and follows us when we have gone from the speakers—a plague sure to spring up in future resurrection."

If young men are wisely influenced and directed, and conscientiously exert their own free energies, they will seek the society of those better than themselves, and strive to imitate their example. In companionship with the good, growing natures will always find their best nourishment; while companionship with the bad will only be fruitful in mischief. There are persons whom to know is to love, honour, and admire; and others whom to know is to shun and despise. Live with persons of elevated characters, and you will feel lifted and lighted up in them; "Live with wolves," says the Spanish proverb, "and you will learn to howl." SAMUEL SMILES.

Flee youthful lusts; but follow Righteousness, faith, charity.

Keep thy heart with all diligence.

Serve the Lord with gladness.

ASPIRATIONS OF YOUTH.

HIGHER, higher, will we climb
   Up the mount of glory,
That our names may live through time
   In our country's story;
Happy, when her welfare calls,
He who conquers, he who falls.

Deeper, deeper, let us toil
   In the mines of knowledge;
Nature's wealth, and learning's spoil,
   Win from school and college;
Delve we there for richer gems
Then the stars of diadems.

Onward, onward, may we press
   Through the path of duty;
Virtue is true happiness,
   Excellence true beauty.
Minds are of celestial birth,
Make we then a heaven of earth.

Closer, closer, let us knit
   Hearts and hands together,
Where our fireside comforts sit,
   In the wildest weather;
O, they wander wide who roam
For the joys of life from home.
             JAMES MONTGOMERY.

Ponder the path of thy feet.

Speak not evil one of another.

Trust in Him at all times.

Order gave each thing view.

THE VALUE OF METHOD.

ONE great advantage which results to the orderly man from his punctual habits of method is, that his energies are never wasted or frittered away. He husbands his strength till the appointed time; calmly meets the difficulty, or the laborious task, at the moment fixed upon as the fittest for coping with its obstacles, and resolutely applying his well-arranged powers, a thing which to the disorderly, hurried, unmethodical and undecided man would appear an almost insurmountable difficulty, yields before him like water to the vessel's prow. Look at the ship, becalmed and without a pilot, with sluggish sails flapping against the mast, swayed alternately by wind or tide, ever in motion, and yet never nearing its destined port. Just such is the irresolute man. Every breeze that blows makes him its sport, and every turn of the tide of fortune finds him dragging helplessly along in its current. But see the same ship with all its sails bent, a prosperous wind urging it on, the pilot at the helm, the seamen ready, each at his appointed post of duty, and the rude ocean yields to its prow, and flings up its spray unheeded and harmless on its sides. No better picture could be conceived of the man of order, method, and punctual

Error eateth like a cancer.

Look difficulties in the face.

Method makes money.

decision. The wind changes—in a moment all hands are ready, the ship is brought about, the sails are set anew; and, moving on a different tack, but with the same port in view, the gallant ship dashes onward in its course.

Hopefulness of Youth.

THIS world is a scene of toils and difficulties, and the meed of earth, be it gain, renown, place, or power, can be secured only by stern labour. There is so much to dishearten, oppress, and keep down the soul, that it needs a constant and ever-accumulating force to sustain and brace our energies. God has placed this vital power eminently in the hearts of our young men. He has gifted them with a strong hope. Let the present be dark as it may, they see always the glimmering rays of a coming light. Let a new era be announced for suffering humanity, and their hearts leap forth to greet the glad future. Selfishness has not yet dimmed their native vision; cold words have not chilled their early glow; the sneer of the sceptic, the pride of the haughty, the frowns of an iron-clad past, the sordid interests of the present, have not yet frozen over their inner life-current.

Justice before Generosity.

WHILE you are generous, see to it that you are also just. Do not give away what does not belong to you. Let us warn you, on account of its moral bearings, against getting into debt. Nothing more effectually robs a man of his best energies, takes the bloom from his cheeks, the glitter from his eyes, the peace from his pillow, than pecuniary indebtedness. And that is not all, nor the worst—debt robs a man of his honesty. Avoid all meanness, but shun as a pestilence the habit of running recklessly and needlessly into debt. Let your expenses be always within your income. If your means are limited, let your outlay and expenditure be correspondingly proportioned to it. Guard against small expenses; it is "the little foxes that spoil the vines," and "the last straw that breaks the camel's back." Buy only what you need, pay what you purchase, and if you are unable to do so, do without it altogether—it may be a temporary privation, but it is the best way in the end. Let "No credit" be your motto, and adhere faithfully to it. Debt leads to extravagance, to fraud, to forgery, to crime of every description, and not unfrequently has driven men to self-destruction.

Sanctions in Favour of Morality.

TIMOTHY THOUGHTLESS and Walter Wise were fellow-apprentices. Thoughtless gave in to the vice of drunkenness; Wise abstained from it. Mark the consequence.

1. Physical sanction. For every debauch, Thoughtless was rewarded by sickness in the head. To recruit himself he lay in bed the next morning, and his whole frame became enervated by relaxation; and when he returned to his work, his work ceased to be a source of satisfaction to him.

Walter Wise refused to accompany him to the drinking table. His health had not been originally strong, but it was invigorated by temperance. Increasing strength gave zest to every satisfaction he enjoyed: his rest at night was tranquil, his risings in the morning cheerful, his labour pleasurable.

2. Social sanction. Timothy had a sister, deeply interested in his happiness. She reproved him at first, then neglected, then abandoned him. She had been to him a source of great pleasure—it was all swept away.

Walter had a brother who had shown indifference to him. That brother had watched over his conduct, and began to show an interest in his well-being—the interest increased from day to day. At last he became a constant visitor, and a more than common friend, and did a thousand services for his brother which no other man in the world would have done.

3. Popular sanction. Timothy was member of a club, which had money and reputation. He went thither one day in a state of inebriety; he abused the secretary, and was expelled by a unanimous vote.

The regular habits of Walter had excited the attention of his master. He said one day to his banker, "The young man is fitted for a higher station." The banker bore it in mind, and, on the first opportunity, took him into his service. He rose from one distinction to another, and was frequently consulted on business of the highest importance by men of wealth and influence.

4. Legal sanction. Timothy rushed out from the club whence he had been so ignominiously expelled. He insulted a man in the streets, and walked penniless into the open country. Reckless of everything, he robbed the first traveller he met. He was apprehended, prosecuted, and sentenced to transportation.

Walter had been an object of approbation to his fellow-citizens. He was called, by their good opinion, to the magistracy. He reached its highest honours, and even sat in judgment on his fellow-apprentice, whom time and misery had so changed that he was not recognised by him.

Beware of evil.

5. Religious sanction. In prison, and in the ship which conveyed Timothy to Botany Bay, his mind was alarmed and afflicted with the apprehension of future punishment — an angry and avenging Deity was constantly present to his thoughts, and every day of his existence was embittered by the dread of the Divine Being.

To Walter the contemplation of futurity was peaceful and pleasurable. He dwelt with constant delight on the benign attributes of the Deity, and the conviction was ever present to him that it must be well, that all ultimately must be well, to the virtuous. Great, indeed, was the balance of pleasure which he drew from his existence, and great was the sum of happiness to which he gave birth.

JEREMY BENTHAM.

THE VALUE OF ENERGY.

WITHOUT this distinguishing mark of true manhood, we fail in securing either the happiness of ourselves or of others. Without Energy a man becomes a drone in society, a nonentity in the world. There are special occasions in the life of every man when he requires to fall back upon the natural energy latent in his nature. Do afflictions, sad and grievous, weigh

In no wise speak against the truth.

Be not overcome of evil,

him down, and seem to crush him to the earth? Let him remember that this is but the "cup" which his Divine Master has given him to drink, the "furnace" which is to try him, and fit him for the life which is to come. Rise, then, afflicted man! Put forth the energy you possess, and soar above your sorrows. Perhaps your business cares are such as to cause you many anxious days and sleepless nights. The times are hard, business is stagnant, and money to meet your engagements difficult to procure; and you feel inclined, nay, compelled, to give way to despair. We hear of such cases every day. Do not look on the dark side of the picture! Keep moving! If you fail of success in one place or transaction, try others, and give yourself no rest till you triumph. The world is large enough for us all. Remember that it does not contain a briar or a thorn that could well be spared. These metaphorical briars and thorns which encompass you, are but instruments to try the energy of your character, and settle your capacity to fulfil the mission of life. To all then we say, suffer no feeling of despondency to weigh you down. Rise triumphantly above all your sorrows and troubles, and you will make the world better and happier for having been born in it.

But overcome evil with good.

Men will praise thee

THE TRUE OBJECT OF WEALTH.

WHAT is success to the merchant? We can readily say what it is *not*.

1. It is *not* merely to accumulate a fixed sum, as the ultimatum of his wishes.

2. It is *not* to gain the control of the market.

3. It is *not* to hold the rod of power over banking and other corporations, and a host of clerks, and other subordinates.

4. It is *not* to lay up immense wealth to leave to thankless heirs.

5. It is *not* to ride—like Whittington—in a magnificent coach, with servants in livery before and behind.

6. It is *not* to live in a noble mansion, furnished according to the expensive taste of the most fashionable upholsterer.

7. It is *not* to hoard gold to gloat over with insane idolatry, as a thing too good to use.

8. It is *not* to accumulate and to hold a vast amount of property for selfish enjoyment, with an iron grasp which death alone can relax, and *then* to bequeath it to benevolent institutions for charitable and religious purposes.

When thou doest well for thyself.

He that keepeth understanding shall find good.

He that getteth wisdom loveth his own soul.

Wealth makes wit waver.

9. It is *not* to become a slave to carping care, at the expense of body and mind, heart and soul — wearing out the body, starving the mind, palsifying the heart, and ruining the soul.

1. Mercantile success *does*, to be sure, involve the fact of gaining money.
2. It is a glorious instrument of power, when used to promote the welfare of others.
3. Success secures the approbation of the world; for, as the wise man says, "Men will praise thee when thou doest well for thyself."
4. Success enables the merchant to possess all the means and appliances for his own comfort and that of his family.
5. It secures for him the blessedness of giving— the sweet indulgence of alleviating human suffering.
6. It furnishes the means of encouraging and promoting art, science, literature, morality, and religion.
7. It secures rest from turmoil and anxiety at the close of life, and leisure to look forward to eternity.

CALL upon a man of business upon matters of business, in the hours of business; transact your business, and when you have finished your business, go about your business, in order that the person called upon may attend to his own business.

Go not forth hastily to strive.

The wicked shall fall into mischief.

A prating fool shall fall.

One volunteer is worth

Resolution of Soul

ENERGY and force of character are among the first requisites essential to success in business. A man may possess a high degree of refinement, large stores of knowledge, and even a well-disciplined mind, but if he is destitute of this one principle, which may be termed resolution of soul, he is like a watch without a mainspring—beautiful, but inefficient, and unfit for service. Man was never made to act the part of an automaton, or mere machine. His powers are not designed to move quite so mechanically. He is to act, as well as to be acted upon. He must give life and stimulus to his calling. Is he not endued with a life-giving power, whose emanation is referred to that original source whence alone can be derived all inspiration? Man's efficiency must give character to his business. That employment upon which is stamped the impress of a living and energetic soul will do honour to any man, in any place, or at any age. It is poor policy, indeed, to loiter till driven by force. We thereby lose all the pleasures of satisfaction. Voluntary service, urged forward by a determined purpose, will give hopeful assurance if not a full warrant of success, and all the happiness

Action is the test of the soul.

Idleness is a canker which destroyeth.

Twenty pressed men.

Action, action, action!

of a just conquest. Behold the sluggish man! His occupation is a worthy one, but it finds him unworthy of the trust. It presses upon him with all the demand of imperative necessity. It finds him but a drone. He is confused by a multiplicity of cares. He is pressed down by a crowd of responsibilities, but makes no generous effort to discharge one of them. Thus his occupation suffers, his family are in want, and that good name, which is better than great riches, is lost. True, man is said to be a creature of circumstances, and he ought to be, in a sense, subject to the superintendence of a leading Providence; but this does not justify inertness of character. Man, by his own decision of character and determined spirit, can do much to remove and surmount the inconveniences and barriers incident to human life. Then be resolute, and both you and your business will go on and prosper.

ACTION AND IDLENESS.

ACTION is really the life, business, and test of the soul; but idleness offers up a similar soul as a blank to the Evil One, for him to write his name upon.

SOUTH.

There is nothing worth doing,

How to Rise in the World.

THE young should begin life with a standard of excellence before them, to which they should readily conform themselves. There should be a fixed determination to make the best of one's self, in whatever circumstances we may be placed. Let the young man determine that whatever he undertakes he will do well; that he will make himself master of the business upon which he enters, and always prepare himself for advancement by becoming worthy of it. It is not opportunity of rising which is wanting, so much as the ability to rise. It is not the patronage of friends and the outward helps of fortune, to which the prominent men of our country owe their elevation, either in wealth or influence, so much as to their own vigorous and steady exertions. We hear a great many complaints, both among young men and old, of the favouritism of fortune, and the partiality of the world; but observation leads us to believe that, to a very great extent, those who deserve promotion obtain it. Those who are worthy of confidence will have confidence reposed in them. Those who give evidence of ability and industry will find opportunity enough for their exercise.

Take time by the forelock.

"Start too late" never wins the race.

Which is not worth doing well.

Do thy work with all diligence,

Take a familiar illustration. A young man engages in some business, and is, in every respect, a beginner in life. A common education is all that he possesses. He knows almost nothing of the world, and very little of the occupation on which he has entered. He performs his duty from day to day sufficiently well, and does what he is expected to do. But it does not enter into his mind to do anything beyond what is required, nor to enlarge his capacities by reading or reflection. He is, at the best, a steady plodding man, who will go forward, if at all, very slowly, and will rise, if at all, to no great elevation. He is not the sort of person who is looked for to occupy a higher position. One opportunity of advancement after another may come directly within his reach, and he asks the influence of friends to help him to secure it. They give their aid feebly, because they have no great hopes of success, and are not confident of their own recommendation. As a matter of course, some one else, more competent or more in earnest, steps in before him, and then we hear renewed complaints of favouritism and injustice. Such an one may say in his defence that he has been guilty of no dereliction of duty; that no fault has been found with him, and that, therefore, he was entitled to advancement. But this does not follow. Something more than that may reasonably be required. To bestow increased confidence, we require

An hypocrite with his mouth destroyeth his neighbour.

Put away from thee a froward mouth.

Honesty, and devotion.

Friends are like fiddle-strings:

the capacity and habit of improvement in those whom we employ. The man who is entitled to rise is one who is always enlarging his capacity, so that he is evidently able to do more than he is actually doing.

In every department of business, whether mechanical or mercantile, or whatever it may be, there is a large field of useful knowledge which should be carefully explored. An observing eye and an inquiring mind will always find enough for examination and study. It may not seem to be of immediate use —it may have nothing to do with this week's or this year's duty — yet it is worth knowing. The mind gains vigour by the inquiry, and the hand itself gains greater skilfulness by the intelligence which directs it.

The result is all the difference between a mere drudge and an intelligent workman; between the mere salesman or clerk, and the enterprising merchant; between the obscure and pettifogging lawyer, and the sagacious, influential counsellor. It is the difference between one who deserves to be, and will be, stationary in the world, and one who, having determined to make the best of himself, will continually rise in influence and true respectability. This whole difference we may see every day among those who have enjoyed nearly equal opportunities. We may allow something for what are called the accidents of social influence, and the turns of fortune.

Let thy heart be in thy work.

Observation of others aids experience.

They may be screwed too tight.

A willing mind makes a ready hand.

But, after all fair allowance has been made, we shall find that the great cause of difference is in the men themselves. Let the young man who is beginning life put away from him all notions of advancement without desert. A man of honourable feelings will not even desire it. He will neither shrink from engaging in duties which he is not able fairly to perform. He will, first of all, secure to himself the capacity of performing them, and then he is ready for them whenever they come.

A Good Rule.

A MAN, who became very rich, was very poor when he was a boy. When asked how he got his riches, he replied: "My father taught me never to play till my work was finished, and never to spend my money till I had earned it. If I had but an hour's work in the day, I must do that the first thing, and in half an hour. After this I was allowed to play; and I then could play with much more pleasure than if I had the thought of an unfinished task before my mind. I early formed the habit of doing everything in time, and it soon became perfectly easy to do so. It is to this I owe my prosperity." Let every boy who reads this go and do likewise.

Put away all childish things.

Man proposes, God disposes.

Work first, play afterwards.

Labour is worship.

WORK, WORK!

I HAVE seen and heard of people who thought it beneath them to work—to employ themselves industriously in some useful labour. Beneath them to work! Why, work is the great motto of life; and he who accomplishes the most by his industry, is the most truly great man — ay, and is the most distinguished man among his fellows, too. And the man who so far forgets his duty to himself, his fellow-creatures, and his God—who so far forgets the great blessings of life, as to allow his energies to stagnate in inactivity and uselessness, had better die; for, says the Holy Writ, "He that will not work, neither shall he eat." An idler is a cumberer of the ground; a weariness and curse to himself, as well as to those around him. *Beneath human beings to work!* Look in the artist's studio, the poet's garret, where the genius of Immortality stands ready to seal his works with her ineffaceable signet, and then you will only see Industry standing by her side. *Beneath human beings to work!* What but work has tilled our fields, clothed our bodies, built our houses, raised our churches, printed our books, cultivated our minds and souls? "*Work* out your own salvation," says the inspired apostle to the Gentiles.

Work is the best medicine.

Labour is the lot of man.

In all labour there is profit.

Remember the Sabbath day

REMEMBER THE SABBATH DAY.

LET the young man form early, and never intermit, the habit of regular attendance on public worship. Why spend the whole of God's day of rest in frivolous conversation, or in habits which enervate the body, and enfeeble, if they do not vitiate, the mind? A young man should attend church, independently of any special good he may derive from the service or the sermon. "I always go to church," said a young man, "even when I am where I do not care for the preacher, and I find the beneficial influence of it on my mind and character." George Washington was always constant in his attendance at the sanctuary. If he had guests living with him, he would take up his hat at the sound of the church bell, and say to his friends, "It is my invariable practice to attend Divine service. I shall be happy in your company if you desire to join me." Some imagine it to be a matter of perfect indifference whether they go to church or remain at home. But public worship is no arbitrary institution. It is not only enjoined in the Bible, but, like society, government, language, and the arts, it has its roots in human nature. Man is a religious being, and he is also a social being. What, then,

In God's house there is pleasure and profit.

The way of the righteous is made plain.

To keep it holy.

A Sabbath well spent

more natural than these hours of mingled praise and prayer? Some think the Sabbath a day for lying in bed, and otherwise pampering the body. Some regard it as a day for walking, riding, or working in the garden; and others think the man of toil may spend it in idleness and dissipation. But though we give the day to physical inactivity, we can and should find a true rest in employing the heart in religious exercises, and the mind in profitable reading.

There is an alarming disease that may be called Sunday sickness, which comes on Saturday evening, rages through the system all day Sunday, and does not intermit its terrible work until breakfast is over on Monday. Then, happily for the patient, it usually vanishes as suddenly as it came. It is seldom, we believe, physically fatal, but it is morally, religiously, and intellectually injurious to human character, and fatal to all church-going.

The weather, too, has an appalling power on the Sabbath. It can be encountered on the week-day; but who can meet a storm, or even the prospect of one, on this day? Wind and rain and snow will not prevent us visiting the theatre, or attending a party at a friend's house, or a public concert, no matter how far distant these meetings may be held from our own residence; but it must never be expected that we should run the slightest risk of getting cold by attending church! We think he would be a moral

Six days shalt thou labour.

Sunday doing leads to ruin.

Brings a week of content.

benefactor to his race, if a man could persuade his fellows that there is really no more danger in venturing out to church on a bright Sunday morning than in attending a crowded, heated meeting on a Saturday night. It would send fulness to many an empty pew, and give joy to many a disheartened preacher.

DUTIES OF DAILY LIFE.

IT is a great misfortune that people so commonly amuse themselves with idle and imaginary schemes, how they would behave, and what they would do, were they in such or such a situation. They would be very good and very exemplary were they very great, very learned, very wealthy, very retired, very old, and the like. But they neglect the gift which is in them, and the work which is appointed for them, while they are thinking of that which is not. Alas! that men's thoughts should be so taken up with dreams and reveries, how they would manage were they in another station, while the chief wisdom of life consists in the assiduous discharge of those duties which belong to their own proper calling.

TUCKER.

Poverty is no crime.

MORAL COURAGE.

HAVE the courage to discharge a debt while you have the money in your pocket.

Have the courage to do without that which you do not need, however much you may admire it.

Have the courage to speak your mind when you should do so, and to hold your tongue when it is better that you should be silent.

Have the courage to speak to a poor friend in a threadbare coat, even in the street, and when a rich one is nigh. The effort is less than many take it to be, and the act is worthy of a king.

Have the courage to set down every penny you spend, and add it up weekly.

Have the courage to admit that you have been in the wrong, and you will remove the fact from the mind of others, putting a desirable impression in the place of an unfavourable one.

Have the courage to adhere to a first resolution when you cannot change it for a better, and to abandon it at the eleventh hour upon conviction.

Have the courage to face a difficulty, lest it kick you harder than you bargain for. Difficulties, like thieves, often disappear at a glance.

Admission of error prevents commission.

Forsake not a friend in adversity.

Be ever open to conviction.

Temperance conduceth to longevity.

Keep the head and feet warm,

And the rest will take no harm.

Have the courage to leave a convivial party at a proper hour for so doing, however great the sacrifice; and to stay away from one, upon the slightest grounds for objection, however great the temptation to go.

Have the courage to dance, if you wish to do so; and to decline dancing, if you dislike the performance, or cannot accomplish it to your satisfaction.

Have the courage to shut your eyes on the prospect of large profits, and to be content with small ones.

Have the courage to tell a man why you will not lend him your money; he will respect you more than if you tell him you can't.

Have the courage to cut the most agreeable acquaintance you possess, when he convinces you that he lacks principle. "A friend should bear with a friend's infirmities"—not his vices.

Have the courage to wear your old garments till you can afford to pay for new ones.

Have the courage to pass the bottle without filling your glass, when you have reasons for so doing; and to laugh at those who urge you to the contrary.

Have the courage to wear thick boots in winter.

Have the courage to review your own conduct; to condemn it where you detect faults; to amend it to the best of your ability; to make good resolves for your future guidance, and to keep them.

Bad principle is worse than no principle.

Avoid all games of chance.

Have the courage to decline playing at cards for money, when " money is an object ;" or to cease playing, when your losses amount to as much as you can afford to lose.

Have the courage to prefer propriety to fashion—one is but the abuse of the other.

Have the courage to confess ignorance whenever, or with regard to whatever subject, you really are uninformed.

Pleasures of Active Life.

None so little enjoy life, and are such burdens to themselves, as those who have nothing to do. The active only have the true relish of life. He who knows not what it is to labour, knows not what it is to enjoy. Recreation is only valuable as it unbends us; the idle know nothing of it. It is the exertion that renders rest delightful, and sleep sweet and undisturbed. That the happiness of life depends on the regular prosecution of some laudable purpose, or lawful calling, which engages, helps, and enlivens all our powers, let those bear witness who, after spending years in active usefulness, retire to enjoy themselves—their life becomes a burden to them.

JOY.

Be always learning.

Never break a promise.

ECONOMY IN KNOWLEDGE.

OLD-FASHIONED economists will tell you never to pass an old nail, or an old horse-shoe, or buckle, or even a pin, without picking it up; because, although you may not want it now, you will find a use for it some time or other. I say the same thing to you with regard to knowledge. However useless it may appear to you at the moment, seize upon all that is fairly within your reach; for there is not a fact within the whole circle of human observation, nor even a fugitive anecdote that you read in a newspaper or hear in conversation, that will not come in play some time or other; and occasions will arise when they will, involuntarily, present their dim shadows in the train of your thinking and reasoning, as belonging to that train, and you will regret that you cannot recall them more distinctly.

WILLIAM WIRT.

ONE broken promise creates twenty doubts; therefore, a man should thoroughly consider what he undertakes before he makes a promise; but, having undertaken it, nothing should prevent him from fulfilling it.

Live peaceably with all men.

Even fragments of knowledge are useful.

Be careful in making promises.

Moral Rectitude.

A MAN of business should be a man of strict moral integrity. This is of indispensable importance, although unfortunately it does not necessarily follow the possession of business habits. Many men of excellent business habits are known to be utterly devoid of all principle of moral rectitude, and of that integrity which is as important for the maintenance and advancement of truth, as for the safe-keeping of our own and our neighbour's property and good name. One-half of the evils, the confusion, and misunderstanding which prevail in the world arises from the suppression and perversion of the truth, from a selfish and jealous distrust of the actions of our fellow-creatures, and from a desire to overreach and rise above them. But that principle of moral rectitude more especially alluded to at present, as essential to the character of a man of business, is comprised in the two commands, "Thou shalt not steal," "Thou shalt not bear false witness." His success depends much upon the extent to which these precepts are observed. His character rises and falls in public estimation in proportion to the acknowledged honesty and uprightness of his dealings; and although he may, for a period, be

Whatsoever a man soweth,

apparently successful in a career of fraud and chicanery, the effect of such success is but to accelerate and render more signal his final ruin and disgrace. While there may be some departments of business in which strict moral integrity forms no essential ingredient of character, there are others in which it is altogether indispensable—as in banking establishments. Here great regularity and attention must be combined with sterling honesty and integrity, and it is accordingly among the men composing this class of society that these virtues are to be found most extensively and most strongly displayed. Here it is that we find men most thoroughly acquainted with all the business transactions, and often with the private arrangements, of their fellow-men; whose lips are as completely sealed as if they were in the most profound ignorance; who have daily and hourly passing through their hands hundreds and thousands of pounds—the gain, or capital, or industry of others—without exciting one covetous or dishonest thought, even although, as is too much the case, they themselves enjoy but a bare competency. These are virtues that elevate and adorn human nature, while they are, at the same time, indispensable to the welfare and order of society.

A contented mind is a continual feast.

Provide things honest in the sight of all men.

That shall he also reap.

Bear all things.

IMPORTANCE OF FIRMNESS.

THERE is no element of human character so potential for weal or woe as firmness. To the merchant and the man of business it is all-important. Before its irresistible energy the most formidable obstacles become as cobweb barriers in its path. Difficulties, the terror of which causes the timid and pampered sons of luxury to shrink back with dismay, provoke from the man of lofty determination only a smile. The whole history of our race—all nature, indeed—teems with examples to show what wonders may be accomplished by resolute perseverance and patient toil.

It is related of Tamerlane, the terror of whose arms spread through all the Eastern nations, and whom victory attended at almost every step, that he once learned from an insect a lesson of perseverance, which had a striking effect on his future character and success.

When closely pursued by his enemies, as a contemporary writer tells the incident, he took refuge in some old ruins, where, left to his solitary musings, he espied an ant tugging and striving to carry a single grain of corn. His unavailing efforts were repeated sixty-nine times, and at each several time, as soon as

Endure all things.

Believe all things.

Hope all things.

Look always on the sunny side.

he reached a certain point of projection, he fell back with his burden, unable to surmount it; but the seventieth time he bore away his spoil in triumph, and left the wondering hero re-animated and exulting in the hope of future victory.

How pregnant the lesson this incident conveys! How many thousand instances there are in which inglorious defeat ends the career of the timid and desponding, when the same tenacity of purpose would crown it with triumphant success!

Resolution is almost omnipotent. It was well observed by a heathen moralist, that it is not because things are difficult that we dare not undertake them. Be, then, bold in spirit. Indulge no doubts. Shakespeare says truly and wisely—

> "Our doubts are traitors,
> And make us lose the good we oft might win
> By fearing to attempt."

In the practical pursuit of our high aim, let us never lose sight of it in the slightest instance; for it is more by a disregard of small things, than by open and flagrant offences, that men come short of excellence. There is always a right and a wrong; and, if you ever doubt, be sure you take not the wrong. Observe this rule, and every experience will be to you a means of advancement.

Neglect not opportunities.

"Go thyself" is better than "See it done."

Well resolved is half done.

How to Start in Life.

THE first great lesson a young man should learn is that he knows nothing; and the earlier and more thoroughly this lesson is learned, the better it will be for his peace of mind and his success in life. A young man bred at home, and growing up in the light of parental admiration and paternal pride, cannot readily understand how it is that every one else can be his equal in talent and acquisition. If, bred in the country, he seeks the life of the town, he will very early obtain an idea of his insignificance.

This is a critical period in his history. The result of his reasoning will decide his fate. If, at this time, he thoroughly comprehends, and in his heart admits and accepts the fact, that he knows nothing and is nothing; if he bows to the conviction that his mind and his person are but ciphers among the significant and cleanly-cut figures about him, and that whatever he is to be, and is to win, must be achieved by hard work, there is abundant hope of him. If, on the contrary, a huge self-conceit still hold possession of him, and he straightens up to the assertion of his cold and valueless self; or if he sink discouraged upon the threshold of a life of fierce competitions and more manly emulations, he may as well be a dead man. The world has no use for such a man, and he has only to retire, or submit to be trodden upon.

When a young man has thoroughly comprehended the fact that he knows nothing, and that, intrinsically, he is of but little value, the next thing for him to learn is that the world cares nothing for him; that he is the subject of no man's overwhelming admiration and esteem; that he must take care of himself. A letter of introduction may possibly procure him an invitation to tea, and nothing more. If he be a stranger, he will find every man busy with his own affairs, and none to look after him. He will not be noticed until he becomes noticeable, and he will not become noticeable until he does something to prove that he has an absolute value in society. No letter of recommendation will give him this, or ought to give him this.

Society demands that a young man shall be not only somebody, but that he shall prove his right to the title; and it has a right to demand this. Society will not take this matter upon trust—at least, not for a long time, for it has been deceived too often. Society is not very particular what a man does, so that it prove him to be a man; then it will bow to him, and make room for him. I know a young man who made a place for himself by writing an article

Wisdom is glorious,

for a certain review. Nobody read the article, so far as I know, but the fact that he wrote such an article, that it was very long, and that it was published, did the business for him. Everybody, however, cannot write articles for reviews, although every person at some period of his life thinks he can; but everybody, who is somebody, can do something. A man must enter society of his own free will, as an active element, or a valuable component, before he can receive the recognition that every true man longs for. I hold this to be right. A man who is willing to enter society as a beneficiary is mean, and does not deserve recognition.

There is no surer sign of an unmanly and cowardly spirit than a vague desire for help; a wish to depend, to lean upon somebody, and enjoy the fruits of the industry of others. There are multitudes of young men who indulge in dreams of help from some quarter, coming in at a convenient moment, to enable them to secure the success in life which they covet. The vision haunts them of some benevolent old gentleman, with a pocketful of money, a trunkful of mortgages and stocks, and a mind remarkably appreciative of merit and genius, who will, perhaps, give or lend them money with which they will commence life and go on swimmingly. Perhaps his benevolence will take a different turn, and he will educate them. Or, perhaps, with an eye

And never fadeth away

to the sacred profession, they desire to become the beneficiaries of some benevolent institution.

To me, one of the most disagreeable sights in the world is that of a young man with healthy blood, broad shoulders, and good bone and muscle, standing with his hands in his pocket, looking and longing for help. I admit that there are positions in which the most independent spirit may accept of assistance—nay, in fact, as a choice of evils, desire it; but for a man who is able to help himself to desire the help of others in the accomplishment of his plans of life, is positive proof that he has received a most unfortunate training, or that there is a leaven of meanness in his composition that should make him shudder. Do not misunderstand me: I would not inculcate that pride of personal independence which repels in its sensitiveness the well-meant good offices and benefactions of friends, or that resorts to desperate shifts rather than incur an obligation. What I condemn in a young man is the love of dependence, the willingness to be under obligation for that which his own efforts may win.

I have often thought that church societies and kindred organisations do much more harm than good, by inviting into the Christian ministry a class of young men who are willing to be helped. A man who willingly receives assistance, especially if he has applied for it, invariably sells himself to his benefactor, unless that benefactor happen to be a man of sense who is giving absolutely necessary assistance to one whom he knows to be sensitive and honourable. Any young man who will part with freedom and the self-respect that grows out of self-reliance and self-support, is unmanly, neither deserving of assistance nor capable of making good use of it. Assistance will invariably be received by a young man of spirit as a dire necessity—as the chief evil of his poverty.

When, therefore, a young man has ascertained and fully realised the fact that he does not know anything; that the world does not care anything about him; that what he wins must be gained by his own brain and hands, and that while he holds in his own power the means of gaining his own livelihood and the objects of his life, he cannot receive assistance without compromising his self-respect and selling his freedom, he is in a fair position for beginning life. When a young man becomes aware that only by his own efforts can he rise into companionship and competition with the shrewd, sharp, strong, and well-drilled minds around him, he is ready for work, and not before.

DR. J. G. HOLLAND.
("Timothy Titcomb.")

Success.

THE most important element of success is economy—economy of money, and economy of time. By economy we do not mean penuriousness, but merely such wholesome thrift as will disincline us to spend our time or money without an adequate return, either in gain or enjoyment. An economical application of time brings leisure and method, and enables us to drive our business, instead of our business driving us. There is nothing attended with results so disastrous as such a miscalculation of our time and means as will involve us in perpetual hurry and difficulty. The brightest talents must be ineffective under such a pressure, and a life of expedients has no end but penury. Worldly success, however, though universally coveted, can be only desirable in so far as it contributes to happiness; and it will contribute to happiness very little, unless there be cultivated a lively benevolence to every animated being. "Happiness," it has been finely observed, "is in the proportion of the number of things we love, and the number of things that love us." To this sentiment we most cordially subscribe, and we should wish to see it written on the tablet of every heart, and producing its fruits of charity. The man, whatever be his fame, or fortune, or intelligence, who can treat lightly another's woe, who is not bound to his fellow-men by the magic tie of sympathy, deserves, and will certainly obtain, the contempt of humankind. Upon him all the gifts of fortune are thrown away; happiness he has none; his life is a dream, a mere lethargy, without a throb of human emotion; and he will descend to the grave

"unwept, unhonoured, and unsung."

Such a fate is not to be envied; and let those who are intent upon success remember that success is nothing without happiness.

RECREATIONS.

LET your recreations be manly, moderate, seasonable, and lawful: the use of recreation is to strengthen your labour and sweeten your rest. But there are some so rigid or so timorous that they avoid all diversions, and dare not indulge in lawful delights for fear of offending. These are hard tutors, if not tyrants to themselves; whilst they pretend to a mortified strictness, they are injurious to their own liberty, and the liberality of their Maker.

STEELE.

Better not be at all,

Something Left Undone.

LABOUR with what zeal we will,
   Something still remains undone,
Something uncompleted still
   Waits the rising of the sun.

By the bedside, on the stair,
   At the threshold, near the gates,
With its menace or its prayer,
   Like a mendicant it waits;

Waits, and will not go away;
   Waits, and will not be gainsaid:
By the cares of yesterday
   Each to-day is heavier made,

Till at length the burden seems
   Heavier than our strength can bear;
Heavy as the weight of dreams,
   Pressing on us everywhere.

And we stand from day to day
   Like the dwarfs of times gone by,
Who, as Northern legends say,
   On their shoulders held the sky.

                      LONGFELLOW.

God shapes the back for the burden.

Work while it is called to-day.

Than not be noble.

TALE-BEARING.

THE Tale-bearer is at once the most odious and most mischievous of characters; the man with whom no secret is safe; who cannot be at ease till he has it out; who goes from one to another, and from party to party, big with it, and watching his opportunity to introduce it appropriately; and when no such opportunity offers, unable to contain himself any longer, and forcing it in, " in season or out of season."

The propensity to reveal secrets—to a certain degree common to all, though in some discovering its unsubdued power by an unrestrained indulgence—is imputable to different causes. In the first place, we are ever apt to be vain of knowing what others are ignorant of; but this of course cannot be known to others, and can procure no gratification to this vanity, without disclosure. Then, further, we are equally apt to be vain of the confidence reposed in us—of our having been made the confidants of others, and especially when these are persons of any name and notoriety. This is a very self-contradictory vanity; for it is impossible to give indulgence to the propensity inspired by it without, in the very act of doing so, showing that the confidence placed in us, and on which we are pluming ourselves, has been *mis*placed. The very revealing of the secret is an avowal that we should not have been trusted, and a warning against trusting us again.

There are various ways of acting the "talebearer." There is that of *open blabbing*. And this, as it is the simplest, is in truth the least dangerous. The character becomes immediately known; and all who have secrets which they really wish kept will take care to withhold from him.

There is next that of *confidential communication*. The secret-holder affects to look this way and that, to ascertain that no one is within hearing; and then, with many whispered *doubts* whether he is doing right, and whispered *no doubts* that he is perfectly safe with the dear friend to whom he speaks, imparts it in a breath that enters only his solitary ear, as a thing received in the profoundest secrecy, and not, on any account whatever, to go further—to be kept still as the grave; thus setting the example of broken confidence, as the encouragement and inducement to keep it! Then he goes and finds out some other dear friend, with whom the same scene is repeated.

There is that also of *sly insinuation*. The person who has the secret neither openly blabs it, nor confidentially whispers it, but throws out hints of his having it—allusions more or less remote to its nature, by which curiosity is awakened, inquiry stimulated,

Charity envieth not.

and the thing ultimately brought to light; while he who threw out the leading notices plumes himself on his having escaped the imputation of being a tale-bearer. The story was not of his telling! Now these, and whatever others there may be, *are all bad;* the greater the amount of pretension and hypocrisy, so much the worse.

Dr. Wardlaw.

The Use of Opposition.

Opposition maketh a man strong.

Kites fly best against the wind.

A CERTAIN amount of opposition is a great help to man. Kites rise against and not with the wind. Even a head wind is better than a dead calm. Let no man become frightened because of opposition. Opposition is what he wants, and must have, to be good for anything. Hardship is the native soil of manhood and self-reliance. He that cannot abide the storm without flinching or quailing, strips himself in the sunshine, and goes to sleep until the cold chills of the evening overtake him, and he finds himself benumbed and helpless. He who but braces himself to the struggle when the wind blows, gives up when the gale is over, and falls asleep in the stillness which follows.

Competition is the life of trade.

Maxims of Bishop Middleton.

PERSEVERE against discouragements.

Keep your temper.

Employ leisure in study, and always have some work in hand.

Be punctual and methodical in business, and never procrastinate.

Never be in a hurry.

Preserve self-possession, and do not be talked out of a conviction.

Rise early, and be an economist of time.

Maintain dignity without the appearance of pride; manner is something with everybody, and everything with some.

Be guarded in discourse, attentive, and slow to speak.

Never acquiesce in immoral or pernicious opinions.

Be not forward to assign reasons to those who have no right to ask.

Think nothing in conduct unimportant or indifferent.

Rather set than follow examples.

Practice strict temperance; and in all your transactions remember the final account.

Decision and Indecision.

"NEVER put off till to-morrow what can be done to-day," is one of the golden rules of the man of business. Depend upon it, whatever present difficulties urge to procrastination, delay will only increase them. The decided man does the present work at the present time, and is thereby as ready for the next call of duty as is the day-labourer for his appointed task after the mid-day meal, or the night's repose. Yet let not the youthful reader rashly jump to the conclusion that all that is needful is to be in a hurry. The very next source of indecision is the want of deliberation; and to that we would join the want of method and orderly arrangement. The man who rushes to his object, without counting the cost or estimating the means, is like the young unbroken colt which dashes off like the wind, exhausts its inexperienced strength in one violent effort, and dashes blindly against the obstacle which it aims at overleaping; while the well-trained courser husbands its strength, reserves the strain for the right moment of action, and bearing its rider over every obstacle, brings him unexhausted to the goal.

The man of decision plans before he executes. He decides, in fact, on what he is to do, and having so done, he then proceeds calmly and deliberately to execute it. It is your procrastinator who is always in a hurry. Twenty things in hands at once, and in such troubled haste to do every one at once—to finish to-day what should have been done yesterday, and to gather up the residue of many delays—that he never has time to do anything well. The first cure for this is to learn to be self-dependent. We must indeed be to some extent controlled by circumstances, but we must also learn to make them subservient to our plans, and to do what should and must be done in spite of obstacles. "You will often," says Foster in his essay on Decision of Character, "see a person anxiously hesitating a long time between different or opposite determinations, though impatient of the pain of such a state, and ashamed of its debility. A faint impulse of preference alternates towards the one, and towards the other; and the mind, while thus held in a trembling balance, is vexed that it cannot get some new thought, or feeling, or motive—that it has not more sense, more resolution, more of anything that would save it from envying even the decisive instinct of brutes. It wishes that any circumstance might happen, or any person might appear, that could deliver it from the miserable suspense.

"In many instances, when a determination *is* adopted, it is frustrated by this indecision. A man,

Be slow in choosing friends:

for example, resolves to make a journey to-morrow, which he is not under an absolute necessity to make, but the inducements appear, this evening, so strong, that he does not think it possible he can hesitate in the morning. In the morning, however, these inducements have unaccountably lost much of their force. Like the sun that is rising at the same time, they appear dim through a mist; and the sky lowers, or he fancies that it lowers; the fatigue appears formidable; and he lingers, uncertain, till an advanced hour determines the question for him, by proclaiming the certainty that it is now too late to go at all."

MAKE YOUR OWN WAY.

THE path of success in business is invariably the path of common-sense. Notwithstanding all that is said about "lucky hits," the best kind of success in every man's life is not that which comes by accident. The only "good time coming" we are justified in hoping for, is that which we are capable of making for ourselves. The fable of the labours of Hercules is indeed the type of all human doing and success. Every youth should early be made to feel that, if he would get through the world usefully and happily, he must rely

One good friend is worth many relations.

Self-reliance is the best reliance.

Be slower in parting with them.

"Now," is yours;

mainly upon himself and his own independent energies. The late Lord Melbourne embodied a piece of useful advice in a letter which he wrote to Lord John Russell, in reply to an application for a provision for one of Thomas Moore's sons.

"My dear John," he wrote, "I return you Moore's letter. I shall be ready to do what you like about it when we have the means. I think whatever is done should be done for Moore himself. This is more distinct, direct, and intelligible. Making a small provision for young men is hardly justifiable; and it is, of all things, the most prejudicial to themselves. They think what they have much larger than it really is; and they make no exertion. The young should never hear any language but this: 'You have your own way to make, and it depends upon your own exertions whether you starve or not.'—Believe me, &c., MELBOURNE."

SAMUEL SMILES.

MANY persons never succeed in their undertakings, from being too indolent to carry out their designs thoroughly. There are others who fail regularly, because, as soon as they find success within their reach, they grow indifferent and give over the attempt. Indolence is a stream that flows slowly on, but surely undermines the foundation of every virtue.

"Then," may never be.

"Now," is the watchword of the wise.

"Now," is on the banner of the prudent.

Business first, pleasure afterwards.

SIR WALTER SCOTT'S ADVICE.

SIR WALTER SCOTT, writing to a young friend who had obtained a situation, gave him this excellent advice :—"You must beware of stumbling over a propensity which easily besets you, from not having your time fully occupied. I mean what the women very expressively call *dawdling*. Your motto must be, *Hoc age*. Do instantly whatever is to be done, and take the hours of recreation after business, and never before it. When a regiment is under march, the rear is often thrown into confusion because the front do not move steadily, and without interruption. It is the same thing with business. If that which is first in hand is not instantly, steadily, and regularly despatched, other things accumulate behind, till affairs begin to press all at once, and no human brain can stand the confusion. Pray, remember this : this is a habit of mind which is very apt to beset men of intellect and talent, especially when their time is not regularly filled up, and is left at their own arrangement. But it is like the ivy round the oak, and ends by limiting, if it does not destroy, the power of manly and necessary exertion. I must love a man so well, to whom I offer such a word of advice, that I will not apologise for it, but expect to hear you are become

Be not too diffident of thyself.

A fool says, "I can't;" a wise man says, "I'll try."

Be always in front of your work.

Pride breeds in great estates,

as regular as a Dutch clock—hours, quarters, minutes, all marked and appropriated. This is a great cast in life, and must be played with all skill and caution."

Conduct towards Inferiors.

NOTHING shows a greater abjectness of spirit than an overbearing temper appearing in a person's behaviour towards inferiors. To insult or abuse those who dare not answer again, is as sure a mark of cowardice as it would be to attack with a drawn sword a woman or a child. Wherever, therefore, you see a person given to insult his inferiors or subordinates, you may assure yourself that he will creep and fawn to his superiors; for the same baseness of mind will lead him to act the part of a bully to those who cannot resist, and of a coward to those who can. But, though servants and other dependents may not have it in their power to retort the injurious usage they receive from their superiors, they are sure to be even with them, by the character they spread abroad of them through the world. Upon the whole, the proper behaviour to inferiors is, to treat them with generosity and humanity; but by no means with familiarity on the one hand, or with insolence on the other.

The abuse of inferiors is cowardice.

Good words cost little, but are worth much.

As worms in sweet fruits.

Fools give up their folly;

A HAPPY LIFE.

OW happy is he born and taught
    That serveth not another's will;
  Whose armour is his honest thought,
    And simple truth his utmost skill!

  Whose passions not his masters are,
    Whose soul is still prepared for death;
  Untied unto the world by care
    Of public fame, or private breath!

  Who envies none that chance may raise,
    Nor vice hath ever understood;
  How deepest wounds are given by praise;
    Not rules of state, but rules of good!

  Who hath his life from rumours freed,
    Whose conscience is his strong retreat;
  Whose state can neither flatterers feed,
    Nor ruin make oppressors great!

  Who God doth late and early pray,
    More of His grace than gifts to lend;
  And entertains the harmless day
    With a religious book or friend!

Wise men never wait for.

TO-MORROW.—The day on which idle men work; Sinners repent and believe; but which

He who is always afraid of falling,

This man is freed from servile hands,
Of hope to rise or fear to fall;
Lord of himself, though not of lands,
And having nothing, yet hath all.

SIR HENRY WOTTON.

THE MAGNANIMOUS MAN.

THE magnanimous man will behave with moderation under both good fortune and bad. He will know how to be exalted and how to be abased. He will neither be delighted with success nor grieved by failure. He will neither shun danger nor seek it, for there are few things which he cares for. He is reticent, and somewhat slow of speech, but speaks his mind openly and boldly when occasion calls for it. He is apt to admire, for nothing is great to him. He overlooks injuries. He is not given to talk about himself or about others; for he does not care that he himself should be praised, or that other people should be blamed. He does not cry out about trifles, and craves help from none.

ARISTOTLE.

Neither shun danger nor seek it.

Beware of entrance to a quarrel.

Does nothing but stumble.

On Suretyship.

"My son, if thou be surety for thy friend, if thou hast stricken thy hand with a stranger, thou art snared with the words of thy mouth, thou art taken with the words of thy mouth."—Prov. vi. 1, 2.

A SURETY is one who becomes security for a debt due by another, in case of the insolvency of the original debtor. In different countries, the customary or legal forms have been different, by which such suretyships are undertaken, and rendered valid. In the first verse allusion is made to the practice of the surety confirming his engagement by giving his hand to the creditor, in presence of witnesses.

Solomon, on different occasions, condemns the practice of suretyship. The condemnation is general. It does not follow, however, that what he says is to be taken as an absolute unqualified prohibition, to which there are no circumstances that can constitute an exception. There are cases in which it is unavoidable; and there are cases in which the law requires it; and there are cases in which it is not only in consistency with law, but required by all the claims of prudence, and justice, and charity; these, however, are rare. And it may be laid down as a maxim regarding the transactions of business, and all the mutual dealings of man with man, that *the less there is of it, the better.* In such cases as the following, it is manifestly inadmissible, and may even in some instances involve a large amount of moral turpitude.

1. It is wrong for a man to come under engagements that are beyond his actually existing means—beyond his ability to pay, in case of need. Such a course is not one merely of imprudence. There is in it a *threefold injustice.* First, to the creditor for whom he becomes security; inasmuch as the security is fallacious, not covering the extent of the risk. Secondly, to his family, if he has one, to whom, in case of the security being required, and the payment called for, the requisition must bring distress and ruin. And thirdly, to those who give him credit in his own transactions, with the risks of his own trade: for, in thus undertaking suretyships, he involves himself, without their knowledge, in the risks of *other* trades besides his own, and thus exposes them to hazards of which, in the outset, they were not aware.

2. The same observations are applicable to the making of engagements with inconsideration and rashness. The case here supposed is evidently that of suretyship *for* a friend *to* a stranger. And the rashness and haste may be viewed in relation either to the *person* or to the *case.*

First, as to the person. The partiality and

In borrowing of money,

warmth of friendship may be a temptation to agree precipitately and without reflection to what both prudence and equity forbid; and especially when the friend presents and presses his suit on the very ground of friendship. That is very trying. How can we refuse an old, attached, and valued friend, or one, it may be, to whose kindness we have been more than once indebted? If a man stands alone, out of business, and without a dependent family, and has, at the same time, abundance of which to dispose, he may be quite at liberty to make such sacrifices to friendship as he pleases. But suppose the reverse of all this—then the claims of justice to others must take precedence of the claims of kindness to the friend. The friend, in such cases, must be regarded not merely in his capacity as a friend, but in his capacity as a man of business. If, for example, he is known to us as a man who is indolent and careless, incorrect and improvident, profuse and extravagant, then, whatever may be our *feelings*, they must on no account be allowed to supersede, in the slightest, the demands of justice. These demands lie against their indulgence, on the part of family and of creditors; whose rights, in such a case, would be clearly and egregiously violated. In such circumstances it is very wrong in your friend to urge you; but, let the urgency be ever so great, and the pain to which you are put ever so excruciating, *right* ought to prevail,

Say "Yes" with caution, "No" with firmness.

Savings, not earnings, make a man rich.

Be precious of thy word.

even if the forfeiture of friendship should be the penalty. Men, when they feel the generous impulse of friendly emotion, and say at once while under it, "I'll be his surety," are exceedingly apt to think at the moment only of themselves, as if the risk were *all their own;* and to forget that in thus hastily "striking hands," they are making creditors and family securities, without asking their consent, or making them aware of the risks.

In the case of the person in whose behalf we bring ourselves under the obligation being "a stranger," the culpability is indefinitely augmented. The young, naturally warm, inexperienced, unsuspecting, and credulous, are very apt to allow themselves to be drawn away by their juvenile ardour, and to commit themselves fast and fondly to new and open-hearted companions. Suretyships "for strangers" are accordingly laid under special condemnation:—"He that is surety for a stranger shall smart for it; and he that hateth suretyship is sure" (Prov. xi. 16). "Take his garment that is surety for a stranger" (Prov. xx. 16). The force of the latter passage is, "If he is your debtor who has come under suretyship for a stranger, you had better see sharply to payment. 'Take his garment' for your debt. He will soon come to it; will soon have nothing more to pay; take in pledge whatever you can get."

It is very far wrong in any man to avail himself

Borrowing lessens credit.

of the claims of friendship to bring another into a situation which, his conscience tells him, is one into which he would not like himself to be drawn; or to induce the friend to do what he knows is either in principle faulty, or in tendency and possible results injurious. This is the very opposite of friendship. It is selfishness betraying friendship, and making it available for its own ends. He who, in business, makes such a use of friendship, exposes himself to just suspicion that all is not right; that he is trying unwarrantable means to prop up a false credit, and to gratify a haste to be rich. It is very natural for us, no doubt, to wish to make our own bargains as secure as possible. But does any man like to be security for the bargains of others? If this is what none like, should any tempt others to do it? Should any one, for the sake of making all sure for himself, seek to place others in circumstances by which *their* security may be affected? Here, as in every case, comes in the golden rule, "All things whatsoever ye would that men should do to you, do ye even so to them." If we cannot trust a man ourselves, so as to transact business with him, would it not be better to forego our bargain, even though it may seem a tempting one, and to decline dealings with him, than to accomplish our purpose by bringing others into a situation we ourselves dislike?

Dr. Wardlaw.

Slow but sure wins the goal.

Hardship is the proper soil for manhood.

Borrowing loses friends.

Be ashamed of idleness.

THE EVILS OF RECKLESSNESS.

YOUTH should be cautioned against a habit of recklessness. If it be perilous to say "I do not care," it is doubly so to rush on with the plea "I did not heed." This is the root of a multitude of transgressions. Let it grow into a habit, and it will undermine the whole character. "He who is idle and frivolous in his apprenticeship," says an author, "will, in nine cases out of ten, turn out a worthless workman; he will stand low as a journeyman, and still lower when he sets up in business for himself." If you do not attend to what lies before you, you can never take advantage of opportunities, and will never do what you engage in to the best of your ability. Many pass through life without even a consciousness of where they are, and what they are doing. They gaze on whatever lies directly before them, "in fond amazement lost."

Human life is a watch-tower. It is the clear purpose of God that every one—the young especially—should take their stand on this tower. Look, listen, learn, wherever you go, wherever you tarry. Something is always transpiring to reward your attention. Let your eyes and ears be always open, and you will often observe, in the slightest incidents, materials of advantage, and means of personal improvement.

A wrathful man stirreth up strife.

Four good words:—

GOOD COUNSEL FOR YOUTH.

Deceit is in the heart of them that imagine evil.

He that regardeth reproof shall be honoured.

D O not be discouraged if, at the outset of life, things do not go on smoothly. It seldom happens that the hopes which we cherish for the future are realised. The path of life appears smooth and level; but when we come to travel upon it, we find it, as it were, very rough and uphill work. The journey is a laborious one; and whether poor or wealthy, high or low, strong or weak, we shall, to our disappointment, find it so. To endure it with as much cheerfulness as possible, and to elbow our way through the great and busy crowd, hoping for little while striving for much, is perhaps the best plan. Do not be discouraged if occasionally you slip down by the way, and your neighbour who follows in your wake treads upon you a little; or, in other words, do not allow one or even two failures to discourage or dishearten you. Accidents will occur, miscalculations will be made, things will turn out totally different from what was expected; and where we looked for a success, we may find only a failure. It is worth remembering that fortune or success is like an April sky, sometimes clear and favourable, and at other times dark and foreboding; and as it would be folly to despair of again seeing the sun because it is stormy to-day, so

Punctuality, Accuracy, Steadiness, Despatch.

The end of learning

it is unwise to sink into despondency when fortune frowns, or troubles arise, since, in the common course of events, she may surely be expected to shine and smile again. Do not be discouraged if you are deceived in the people of the world; they are good and bad certainly, but the bad predominate. From such sources as these you may be most unexpectedly deceived, and you will naturally feel pained under such deceptions; but to these you will become accustomed. If you fare as other older and better people than yourself fare, they will lose their novelty and their effect before you grow grey; and you will learn to trust such circumstances more cautiously, and to examine them more closely, before they are permitted to injure you. Do not be discouraged under any circumstances. Go steadily forward—rather consult and trust in your own conscience when you know that it is right, than in the opinion of others, though the latter is not always to be disregarded. Be industrious, be sober, be honest; deal in perfect kindness and fairness with all who come in contact with you; exercise a friendly and obliging spirit to all whom you have intercourse with; and if you do not prosper so rapidly as your neighbours seem to do, depend upon it that you will be at least as happy.

Whoso walketh uprightly shall be saved.

Be kindly affectioned one to another.

Should be holiness of life.

A heavy burden may be borne

Press Onward.

PERSEVERANCE, dear my lord,
    Keeps honour bright: to have done, is to
       hang
  Quite out of fashion, like a rusty mail,
    In monumental mockery. Take the instant
      way,
For honour travels in a strait so narrow,
Where one but goes abreast: keep, then, the path;
For emulation hath a thousand sons,
That one by one pursue: if you give way,
Or hedge aside from the direct forthright,
Like to an enter'd tide, they all rush by,
And leave you hindmost:
Or, like a gallant horse, fall'n in first rank,
Lie there for pavement to the abject rear,
O'er-run and trampled on: then what they do in
    present,
Though less than yours in past, must o'er-top yours;
For time is like a fashionable host,
That slightly shakes his parting guest by the hand,
And with his arms outstretched, as he would fly,
Grasps in the comer: welcome ever smiles,
And farewell goes out sighing. O let not virtue seek
Remuneration for the thing it was;
For beauty, wit,

Honour travels in a narrow path.

The price of reason is above rubies.

By the help of many shoulders.

The wise in heart

High birth, vigour of bone, desert in service,
Love, friendship, charity, are subjects all
To envious and calumniating time.
SHAKESPEARE.

The Truly Noble Man.

THE man of noble spirit converts all occurrences into experience, between which experience and his reason there is marriage, and the issue are his actions. He moves by affection, not for affection; he loves glory, scorns shame, and governeth and obeyeth with one countenance, for it comes from one consideration. Knowing reason to be no idle gift of Nature, he is the steersman of his own destiny. Truth is his goddess, and he takes pains to get her, not to look like her. Unto the society of men he is a sun, whose clearness directs their steps in a regular motion. He is the wise man's friend, the example of the indifferent, the medicine of the vicious. Thus time goeth not from him, but with him, and he feels age more by the strength of his soul than by the weakness of his body. Thus feels he no pain, but esteems all such things as friends that desire to file off his fetters and help him out of prison.
SIR THOMAS OVERBURY.

It is better to receive the rebuke of the wise, *Than for a man to hear the song of fools.*

Will receive commandments.

Let thy word be as a bond.

KEEP OUT OF DEBT.

THE honourable man is frugal of his means, and pays his way honestly. He does not seek to pass himself off as richer than he is, or, by running into debt, open an account with ruin. As that man is not poor whose means are small but whose desires are controlled, so that man is rich whose means are more than sufficient for his wants. When Socrates saw a great quantity of riches, jewels, and furniture of great value carried in pomp through Athens, he said, "Now do I see how many things I do *not* desire." "I can forgive everything but selfishness," said Perthes. "Even the narrowest circumstances admit of greatness with reference to 'mine and thine;' and none but the very poorest need fill their daily life with thoughts of money, if they have but prudence to arrange their housekeeping within the limits of their income."

A man may be indifferent to money because of higher considerations, as Faraday was, who sacrificed wealth to pursue science; but if he would have the enjoyments that money can purchase, he must honestly earn it, and not live upon the earnings of others, as those do who habitually incur debts which they have no means of paying. When Magion,

Stand not on gentility.

always drowned in debt, was asked what he paid for his wine, he replied that he did not know, but he believed they "put something down in a book." This "putting-down in a book" has proved the ruin of a great many weak-minded people, who cannot resist the temptation of taking things upon credit which they have not the present means of paying for; and it would probably prove of great social benefit if the law which enables creditors to recover debts contracted under certain circumstances were altogether abolished. But, in the competition for trade, every encouragement is given to the incurring of debt, the creditor relying upon the law to aid him in the last extremity. When Sydney Smith once went into a new neighbourhood, it was given out in the local papers that he was a man of high connections, and he was besought on all sides for his "custom." But he speedily undeceived his new neighbours. "We are not great people at all," he said; "we are only common honest people—people that pay our debts."

Hazlitt, who was a thoroughly honest though rather thriftless man, speaks of two classes of persons, not unlike each other—those who cannot keep their own money in their hands, and those who cannot keep their hands from other people's. The former are always in want of money, for they throw it away on any object that first presents itself, as if to get rid of it; the latter make away with what they have of

Read to understand.

their own, and are perpetual borrowers from all who will lend to them; and their genius for borrowing, in the long run, usually proves their ruin.

SAMUEL SMILES.

ADVANTAGES OF READING.

IF I were to pray for a taste which should stand me in stead under every variety of circumstances, and be a source of happiness and cheerfulness to me through life, and a shield against its ills, however things might go amiss, and the world frown upon me, it would be a taste for reading. I speak of it, of course, only as a worldly advantage, and not in the slightest degree as superseding or derogating from the higher office, and surer and stronger panoply, of religious principles; but as a taste, an instrument, and a mode of pleasurable gratification. Give a man this taste, and the means of gratifying it, and you can hardly fail of making a happy man, unless indeed you put into his hands a perverse selection of books. You place him in contact with the best society in every period of history—with the wisest, the wittiest, with the tenderest, the bravest, and the purest characters

Good books nourish the soul.

that have adorned humanity. You make him a denizen of all nations, a contemporary of all ages. The world has been created for him. It is hardly possible but that the character should take a higher and better tone from the constant habit of associating in thought with a class of thinkers, to say the least of it, above the average of humanity. It is morally impossible but that the manners should take a tinge of good-breeding and civilisation from having constantly before one's eyes the way in which the best-bred and the best-informed men have talked and conducted themselves in their intercourse with each other. There is a gentle but perfectly irresistible coercion in a habit of reading, well directed, over the whole tenor of a man's character and conduct, which is not the less effectual because it works insensibly, and because it is really the last thing he dreams of. It cannot, in short, be better summed up than in the words of the Latin poet:—

" Emollit mores, nec sinit esse feros."

It civilises the conduct of men, and suffers them not to remain barbarous.

Sir John Herschel.

He that cheats in jesting,

Hasting to be Rich.

AN undue haste to become rich is a great moral danger to youth. Time was when a young man would commence business with a small capital, but which was all his own; be content to buy goods only when he could pay for them; do business with responsible customers; be satisfied with moderate gains and a humble establishment, graduating his expenses by his income. But, step by step, this good old path has been deserted. Young men now commence business with an overgrown stock, purchased on credit; they trust all men, and to any extent; engage a costly warehouse, and adorn it with rich fittings; give elegant and expensive parties; and live in all respects, not according to their actual means and resources, but either on the property of others, or on some imaginary mine of wealth which is to be accumulated in the future. And what is the result? Bankruptcy, chancery, ruin-making profits out of a compromise with deluded and hapless creditors. If the law of man shields such transactions, we know well, as sure as there is a God in heaven, that He must frown on the act and the actor. The desire to be rich lies at the basis of the long array of defalcations, frauds, and embezzlements, of which the

Will not be honest in earnest.

Ill-got wealth never prospered.

journals of the day give such frequent and fearful disclosures. The clerk, aspiring to be wealthy, takes money from the desk of his employer. We are startled by announcements of some church officer or corporation treasurer, or some bank cashier, detected in a career which dates back through long years of artful stratagems employed to abstract money from the funds in charge, to meet the outlay of extravagance and vice. Some otherwise good man, tempted, it may be, by the chance of an apparently successful investment, is arraigned before a court of justice; and, through some loophole in the meshes of the great net of the law, he is suffered to escape his deserts, and becomes the recipient of a wide-spread sympathy and forgiveness.

BEGINNING LIFE.

WHEN a youth enters a workshop, warehouse, or office, he begins a work whose moral issues thought cannot span. In the first place, he is to learn there the great art of accumulation—he is to enter on the ascending grade of a business life. To make sure of gain and competency, he must set out right. "Be not slothful in business," says the Preacher. Industry,

Let duty be your pride.

To thine own self be true.

Wilful waste makes woeful want.

Between the joinings of the stones,

the demand of God, is also the germ of all permanent success in this world; and therefore, for his own sake, a youth will put his hand resolutely and steadily to the stern tasks of a diligent labour.

For his employer's sake he will cherish an immaculate honesty. We do not here refer to shunning the gross crime of taking money or goods by stealth. That is not the chief temptation in this way. We advert to the thousand little acts of dishonesty which are the leading-strings to all the larger ones. The impression often prevails that none but a skilful eye can detect these things. It is not so: the employer, though he should not discover each specific act of dishonesty, does, sooner or later, perceive the general spirit of unfaithfulness in one who serves him with no conscience and no heart. Equally, and as surely, does he observe every token of fidelity and honesty. Be always early at your post, and late to leave it; save in little things for your employer, just as you would for yourself; make his interest your interest. In this way you soon gain his confidence. Step by step you become indispensable to him; he increases your compensation, makes you an occasional present, promotes you over others—the idle and the unfaithful—and eventually, perhaps, makes you his partner.

And that is not all; you form, in this way, the very best habits of business; and whenever and wherever you come to act for yourself, you are sure

Let conscience guide your conduct.

Diligent in business, fervent in spirit,

of success. Fidelity in small things, that is the right arm of all true power and progress—it is the corner-stone of prosperity, as in character, so in business.

DILIGENCE IN BUSINESS.

CULTIVATE a spirit of diligence, both in your temporal and spiritual employ. Strictly adhere to your business: religion commands this. There may be difficulties in your calling, and so there are in every situation; but let not this relax your exertions, lest you give occasion for the enemy to speak ill of you. Besides, assiduity in your lawful concerns is one of the best ways to be preserved from temptation. Idleness has led to a thousand evil consequences; while, in itself, it is a most unhappy state of mind to labour under. It is good to be employed. Action is really the life, business, and rest of the soul. "Idleness," as South says, "offers up the soul, as a blank to the devil, for him to write what he will upon it." Idleness is the emptiness, and business the fulness, of the soul; and we all know that we may infuse what we will into empty vessels, but a full one has no room for a further infusion.

BUCK.

Idleness is fraught with evil.

Industry is pregnant with good.

Serving the Lord.

Sow good works and

NEVER BE IDLE.

IT is the neglect of the odds and ends of our time, that are frittered away, or allowed to slip uselessly past, that is the cause of much of our moral unsoundness and corruption. A dead fly, little thing as it is, will spoil a whole box of the most precious ointment; and idleness, if it be once suffered, though but for a brief time, is sure, by the communication of its listless quality, to clog and cumber the clockwork of our whole life. It is the ancient enemy—the old man of the Arabian tales. Once allow him to get upon your shoulders, and no power on earth can shake him off again.

I had a notion of this truth, and framed my plan after the following rules. I resolved that every minute should be occupied by thought, word, or act, or, if by none of these, by intention; vacancy was my only outcast, the scape-goat of my proscription. For this, my purpose, I required a certain energy of will, as, indeed, this same energy is requisite for every other good thing, of every sort or kind; without it we are as powerless as grubs, noisome as ditch-water, vague, loose, and unpredestinate as the clouds above our heads. However, I had sufficient of this

Work witnesseth the well-doer.

Nothing is impossible to a willing mind.

Reap lasting joys.

Grasp all, lose all.

energy to serve me. I soon felt the excellence of the practice; it penetrated through my entire moral system; I cherished it, and made a point of everything. I was active, brisk, and animated in all things that I did, even to the picking up of a glove, or asking the time of day. If I ever felt the approach of the insidious languor, even in the slightest degree, I at once said to myself, "In the next quarter of an hour I will do such a thing," and, *presto!* it was done, and much more into the bargain; my mind was set in motion, my spirits stirred and quickened, and raised to their proper level. I watched the cloud, and dissipated it at its first gathering, well knowing that, if it could grow but to the size of a man's hand, it would spread out everywhere, and darken my whole horizon.

Oh, that this example might be as profitable to others as the practice has been to myself! How rich would be the reward of this book, if its readers would but take to heart this one article; if the simple truths that it here speaks could prompt them to take their happiness into their own hands, and learn the value of industry, not from what they may have heard of it, but because they have themselves discovered and experienced! In the first place, its direct and inevitable value, inasmuch as it quickens, and cheers, and gladdens every moment that it occupies, and keeps off the evil one, by repelling him at the outposts,

Persevere to the end.

Be anxious for nothing.

instead of admitting him to a doubtful, perhaps a deadly, struggle within the citadel; and, again, its more remote but no less certain value, as the mother of many virtues, when it has once grown into the temper of the mind; and the nursing-mother of many more. And if we gain so much by its entertainment, how much more must we not lose by its neglect?

Our vexations are annoying to us; the disappointments of life are grievous, its calamities deplorable, its indulgences and lusts sinful; but our idleness is worse than all these—more painful, more hateful, and, in the amount of its consequences, if not in its very essence, more sinful than even sin itself— just as the trunk of the tree is more fruitful than any of the branches which spring from it. In fine, do what you will, only do something, and that something actively and energetically. Read, converse, work, play, think, or study; the whole range is open to you, only let your mind be full, or your hands occupied, and you will want little or nothing to complete your happiness.

From "Self-Formation," an American work.

Little by little one goes far.

The biggest horses are not the best travellers.

Little winnings make a heavy purse.

Oaks may fall

INDUSTRY AND INTEGRITY.

THERE is nothing possible to man which industry and integrity will not accomplish. The poor boy of yesterday—so poor that a shilling was a miracle in his vision; houseless and breadless; compelled to wander on foot from village to village, with his bundle on his back, in order to procure labour and the means of subsistence—has become the talented young man to-day, by the power of his good right arm, and the potent influence of his pure principles, firmly and perpetually maintained. When poverty, and what the world calls disgrace, stared him in the face, he shuddered not, but pressed onward, and exulted in high and honourable exertions in the midst of accumulating disasters and calamities. Let the young man be cherished; for he honours his country, and dignifies his race. Wealth!—what cares he for that, as long as his heart is pure, and his walk upright? He knows, and his country knows, and his country tells, that the little finger of an honest and upright young man is worth more than the whole body of an effeminate and dishonest rich man. These are the men who make the country—who bring to it whatever of iron sinew and unfailing spirit it possesses or desires.

When reeds brave the storm.

www.ingramcontent.com/pod-product-compliance
Lightning Source LLC
Chambersburg PA
CBHW031728230426
43669CB00007B/285